WOMEN EDUCATION

Dr. Shubhangi Anant Dongre
M.Sc., M.Ed, NET, SET, Ph.D. (Education)
Associate Professor
Punjabhai Patel College of Education,
Gondia (Maharashtra)

Dr. Kavita Maruti Ghughuskar
M.Sc., M.Ed, SET, Ph.D. (Education)
Associate Professor
Adv. Vitthalrao Hande College of
Education, Nashik (Maharashtra)

Title : Women Education

Author : Dr. Shubhangi Anant Dongre, Dr. Kavita Maruti Ghughuskar

Edition : First (December, 2024)

ISBN : 9789348332943

Published by

Regd. Add.: 254, Khuriyakhatta No. 10, Bindukhatta,

Lalkuan, Nainital - 262402, Uttarakhand, India

Website : www.prachidigital.com

E-mail : info@prachidigital.in

Phone : +91 976041 7980, +91 976041 8103

Printed by :

Manipal Technologies Limited, Bengaluru - 560001, Karnataka

PREFACE

Women's education in India evolves from the longest time- Ancient to the modern age. This book covers women's education and development of women education in India from various dimensions of development. This book also throws light on issues like gender equality, the current position of women in India, women empowerment, the constitutional provisions for women, various schemes for women empowerment, leadership role of women in National Building along with the work of various Indian thinkers in promoting women education with wide range of coverage in depth narration and student friendly presentation. This book will definitely be beneficial for the B. Ed student as well as Teacher Educators. It is also useful to catter the needs of students of UG and PG level education under CBCS pattern. The authors wish to acknowledge the publisher for rapidly accepting to publish this book.

INDEX

CHAPTER - 1

INTRODUCTION TO WOMEN EDUCATION

1. 1 - Need for Women Education

The need for women's education is undeniable and multifaceted. It is not merely a matter of social justice but a critical factor in economic development, health improvement, and societal progress. Despite the challenges, concerted efforts by governments, communities, and international organizations can overcome these barriers. By prioritizing women's education, societies can unlock the full potential of half their population, leading to more prosperous, equitable, and sustainable development. Investing in women's education is, therefore, an investment in the future of humanity.

1. Economic Growth and Development: Educating women is directly linked to economic growth and development. Numerous studies have shown that increasing women's education boosts economic productivity. Educated women are more likely to enter the workforce, leading to a larger, more skilled labor pool. This, in turn, increases household incomes and contributes to national economic development. For example, a World Bank report suggests that each additional year of schooling for girls can increase their future earnings by 10-20%. Furthermore, women tend to reinvest a significant portion of their earnings back into their families and communities, fostering a cycle of prosperity and growth. Educated women are more likely to start and sustain businesses, leading to entrepreneurial growth and innovation.

2. Health Benefits: Education has a profound impact on health outcomes for women and their families. Educated women are better informed about health and nutrition, leading to healthier families. They are more likely to seek medical care, immunize their children, and adopt preventive health measures. Studies indicate that children of educated mothers have higher survival rates and better health metrics. Additionally, women's education is crucial in combating the spread of diseases. For example, educated women are more knowledgeable about HIV/AIDS prevention and are better equipped to make informed decisions regarding their sexual and reproductive health.

3. Reduction in Child Marriages and Fertility Rates: Education is one of the most effective tools in reducing child marriages and controlling fertility rates. Girls with access to education are less likely to marry young and are more likely to have fewer, healthier children. Educated women tend to delay marriage and childbirth, opting instead for career and personal development opportunities. This shift not only improves the quality of life for women but also contributes to the broader goals of population control and sustainable development.

4. Empowerment and Gender Equality: Education empowers women by providing them with the knowledge, skills, and confidence to participate fully in society. It enables women to challenge discriminatory practices and advocate for their rights. Empowered women are more likely to participate in political and civic activities, contributing to more inclusive and democratic governance. Gender equality is not only a fundamental human right but also a cornerstone of a prosperous society. Educated women can break the cycle of poverty and discrimination, leading to a more equitable distribution of resources and opportunities. This, in turn, fosters social cohesion and stability.

5. Positive Social Change: Educating women has a ripple effect on society. Women with education tend to support the education of their children, leading to a more educated future generation. They are also more likely to be involved in community activities, volunteer work, and social initiatives, driving positive change within their communities. Educated women are crucial in challenging and changing harmful cultural practices such as female genital mutilation

(FGM) and gender-based violence. By advocating for their rights and those of others, educated women play a pivotal role in creating a more just and equitable society.

1. 2 - Importance of Women Education

Education for women has historically been fraught with challenges, rooted in deep-seated cultural, social, and economic barriers. Despite these obstacles, the movement towards gender equality in education has gained significant momentum over the past few centuries. Today, the importance of women's education is widely recognized as a critical component of social progress and economic development.

1. Economic Benefits: The economic advantages of educating women are profound. Numerous studies demonstrate that women's education contributes significantly to economic growth. Educated women are more likely to participate in the workforce, bringing diverse skills and perspectives that enhance productivity and innovation. The World Bank reports that each additional year of schooling for girls increases their future earnings by 10-20%, underlining the economic benefits of women's education. Furthermore, women tend to reinvest a substantial portion of their income back into their families and communities, creating a ripple effect that fosters sustainable economic development. This reinvestment often results in better health, nutrition, and educational outcomes for children, thereby breaking the cycle of poverty. Additionally, educated women are more likely to start and sustain businesses, contributing to entrepreneurial growth and economic diversification.

2. Health Improvements: Education significantly impacts health outcomes, both for women and their families. Educated women are better informed about health and nutrition, leading to healthier families and lower child mortality rates. They are more likely to seek medical care, ensure their children are immunized, and adopt preventive health measures. According to research, children of educated mothers have higher survival rates and improved health indicators. Women's education is also crucial in addressing public health issues. For example, educated women are more knowledgeable about HIV/AIDS prevention and other communicable diseases, which is vital in combating the spread of these diseases. Furthermore, education empowers women to make informed decisions regarding their reproductive health, leading to lower fertility rates and better family planning.

3. Social and Cultural Benefits: Educating women leads to significant social and cultural benefits. One of the most important impacts is the reduction of child marriages and early pregnancies. Girls who receive an education are more likely to marry later and have fewer, healthier children. This delay in marriage and childbirth allows women to pursue personal development and career opportunities, improving their overall quality of life. Education also plays a crucial role in challenging and changing harmful cultural practices. Educated women are more likely to advocate against practices such as female genital mutilation (FGM) and gender-based violence. They can serve as role models and leaders within their communities, driving social change and promoting gender equality. By empowering women with knowledge and skills, education helps to dismantle patriarchal norms and create more inclusive societies.

4. Political and Civic Engagement: Women's education is essential for fostering political and civic engagement. Educated women are more likely to participate in political processes, including voting, running for office, and engaging in advocacy work. Their participation brings diverse perspectives and solutions to political discourse, leading to more representative and effective governance. Furthermore, education equips women with the skills and confidence needed to assume leadership roles within their communities and beyond. This increased representation of women in leadership positions is crucial for achieving gender equality and addressing issues that disproportionately affect women. Studies show that when women are involved in decision-making processes, policies and programs are more likely to address social inequalities and promote sustainable development.

5. Reduction of Gender Disparities: Education is a powerful tool for reducing gender disparities across various sectors. In many parts of the world, women and girls face significant barriers to education, including poverty, cultural norms, and safety concerns. Addressing these barriers and ensuring equal access to education is critical for achieving gender equality. Educated women are more likely to advocate for their rights and the rights of others, challenging discriminatory practices and policies. This advocacy is essential for creating a more just and equitable society where women have equal opportunities to succeed. By reducing gender disparities in education, societies can unlock the full potential of their populations, leading to greater innovation, productivity, and social cohesion.

6. Global Development and Sustainability: The importance of women's education extends beyond individual and national benefits to global development and sustainability. The United Nations' Sustainable Development Goals (SDGs) highlight the critical role of education in achieving sustainable development. Goal 4 specifically aims to ensure inclusive and equitable quality education for all, with a focus on eliminating gender disparities. Educating women is fundamental to achieving other SDGs as well, including those related to poverty reduction, health, economic growth, and gender equality. For instance, educated women are more likely to engage in sustainable practices, contribute to environmental conservation, and support initiatives aimed at addressing climate change. By investing in women's education, the global community can make significant strides towards a more sustainable and equitable future.

7. Barriers and Challenges: Despite the clear benefits, numerous barriers to women's education persist. In many developing countries, cultural and social norms prioritize male education, relegating girls to domestic roles. Economic constraints also play a significant role, as families with limited resources may favor educating boys over girls.

Additionally, safety concerns, such as long distances to schools and the threat of violence, deter many girls from attending school. Addressing these challenges requires a multifaceted approach. Governments must implement policies that mandate free and compulsory education for all children, with specific provisions for girls. Financial incentives, such as scholarships and conditional cash transfers, can help alleviate economic barriers. Community engagement and advocacy are also crucial in changing cultural attitudes and practices that limit girls' education.

1. 3 - Objectives of Women Education

1. Empowerment: One of the primary objectives of women education is empowerment. Educating women equips them with the knowledge, skills, and confidence to make informed decisions about their personal and professional lives. Empowered women are more likely to assert their rights, seek opportunities for personal growth, and participate actively in societal development. This empowerment extends to various aspects of life, including health, family planning, and economic activities, thereby fostering a sense of agency and independence. Education helps women to understand and exercise their rights, challenge discriminatory practices, and contribute to the creation of more equitable and just societies.

2. Promotion of Gender Equality: Education plays a crucial role in promoting gender equality. By providing women with equal access to educational opportunities, societies can begin to dismantle long-standing gender norms and stereotypes. Educated women are better positioned to advocate for themselves and other women, challenging systemic inequalities and advocating for policies that promote gender parity. Moreover, education fosters an environment where men and women can interact as equals, which helps in breaking down prejudices and promoting mutual respect. Through education, women can gain the tools needed to challenge and change the traditional roles that have historically limited their participation in various spheres of life.

3. Economic Development: Educating women significantly contributes to economic development. When women are educated, they are more likely to enter the workforce, start their own businesses, and contribute to the economy. This increased participation can lead to higher productivity, innovation, and economic diversification. Additionally, educated women tend to earn higher wages, which can lift families out of poverty and stimulate economic growth. Education also enables women to make more informed financial decisions, manage resources effectively, and contribute to the financial stability of their households. As a result, investing in women's education is not just a matter of social justice but also an economic imperative.

4. Health Improvement: Another critical objective of women education is the improvement of health outcomes. Educated women are more likely to adopt healthier lifestyles, seek medical care when needed, and make informed decisions about their reproductive health. This knowledge translates into lower maternal and infant mortality rates, better child health, and increased life expectancy. Education also empowers women to become health advocates within their communities, spreading awareness about health and hygiene practices. Moreover, educated women are better equipped to understand and mitigate health risks, leading to overall better health outcomes for themselves and their families.

5. Social Development: Women education is a key driver of social development. Educated women are more likely to participate in civic activities, volunteer for community service, and engage in political processes. This participation helps build more democratic, stable, and inclusive societies. Education fosters critical thinking, encourages the questioning of societal norms, and promotes active citizenship. By participating in decision-making processes at various levels, educated women can influence policies and practices that affect their lives and the lives of others. This engagement is essential for creating societies that are responsive to the needs of all their members and for ensuring that women's voices are heard in all spheres of life.

In summary, the objectives of women education encompass empowerment, gender equality, economic development, health improvement, and social development. Achieving these objectives requires a concerted effort from governments, communities, and individuals to ensure that all women have access to quality education and the opportunities it brings. By focusing on these goals, we can create a more just, equitable, and prosperous world for everyone.

1. 4 - Causes for the Focus on Women Education

The focus on women education has been driven by a combination of international development goals, compelling evidence of its positive impacts, and persistent advocacy by women's rights organizations. One of the primary catalysts has been the recognition by global development frameworks, such as the United Nations' Millennium Development Goals (MDGs) and the Sustainable Development Goals (SDGs), that education is a fundamental human right and a critical component of sustainable development. These frameworks have underscored the importance of gender equality in education, prompting countries to prioritize policies and programs that enhance educational access for women and girls. The international community's commitment to these goals has galvanized efforts worldwide to close the gender gap in education.

Evidence of the substantial benefits of women education has further intensified the focus on this issue. Numerous studies have demonstrated that educating women leads to a wide array of positive outcomes, including economic growth, improved public health, and greater social cohesion. For instance, educated women are more likely to participate in the labor market, which boosts economic productivity and innovation. Additionally, they tend to have fewer, healthier children and are better informed about health and nutrition, leading to improved family health and reduced maternal and infant mortality rates. These benefits extend beyond individual families to broader societal gains, as educated women contribute to the development of more stable and prosperous communities. The persistent advocacy by women's rights organizations has also played a crucial role in focusing attention on women education. These organizations have been instrumental in highlighting the barriers that women and girls face in accessing education, such as cultural norms, economic constraints, and discriminatory practices. They have campaigned for policy changes, increased funding for education, and targeted programs that address these barriers. Advocacy efforts have raised public awareness about the importance of women education and have pressured governments and international bodies to take concrete actions to ensure that all women and girls can access quality education.

Moreover, changing economic landscapes and labor market demands have reinforced the need for women education. As economies evolve and become more knowledge-based, the demand for skilled labor has increased. Educating women is essential to meeting this demand and ensuring that half of the population can contribute to and benefit from economic opportunities. In many developing countries, there is a growing recognition that gender inequality in education is a significant impediment to economic development and that investing in women education is crucial for achieving long-term economic growth.

Cultural and social shifts have also contributed to the focus on women education. There is a growing acknowledgment that traditional gender roles, which have often restricted women's access to education, need to be reevaluated. Societies are increasingly recognizing the value of educating women not just for their own empowerment but also for the broader benefits that education brings to families and communities. This shift in cultural attitudes has supported efforts to promote gender equality in education and to challenge norms that limit educational opportunities for women and girls.

In summary, the focus on women education has been driven by

international development goals, compelling evidence of its benefits, persistent advocacy, economic imperatives, and cultural shifts. These factors have converged to create a strong impetus for ensuring that women and girls have equal access to quality education, recognizing that this is essential for achieving broader goals of economic development, public health, and social equity.

1. 5 - Advantages of Women Education

Education is widely recognized as a fundamental human right and a powerful tool for social and economic development. When it comes to the education of women, the advantages extend far beyond individual empowerment, influencing broader societal outcomes in areas such as health, economy, politics, and social cohesion. Educating women yields multifaceted benefits that contribute to the well-being and prosperity of communities and nations alike.

1. Empowerment and Self-Determination: Education serves as a potent vehicle for empowering women, providing them with the knowledge, skills, and confidence to assert their rights and make informed decisions about their lives. Through education, women gain autonomy over their choices, whether it be regarding their education, career, marriage, or reproductive health. By empowering women to take control of their destinies, education breaks the cycle of dependency and vulnerability, fostering self-determination and resilience.

2. Economic Participation and Poverty Alleviation: One of the most significant advantages of educating women is its positive impact on economic development and poverty alleviation. Educated women are more likely to enter the workforce, earn higher incomes, and contribute to household and national economies. Studies have shown that increasing women's education and workforce participation correlates with higher GDP growth rates and greater economic productivity. By harnessing the talents and potential of half the population, societies can unlock new sources of innovation, entrepreneurship, and economic growth.

3. Health and Well-being: Educating women is a crucial determinant of public health outcomes, particularly in areas such as maternal and child health. Educated women are more likely to adopt healthier behaviors, seek prenatal care, and access reproductive health services, leading to reduced maternal mortality rates and improved child health outcomes. Furthermore, educated women are better equipped to make informed decisions about their health and the health of their families, resulting in lower rates of malnutrition, infectious diseases, and preventable illnesses.

4. Gender Equality and Social Justice: Education stands as a cornerstone of gender equality, challenging and dismantling traditional gender norms and stereotypes. By providing equal access to education for both genders, societies can create more inclusive and equitable environments where women have the same opportunities as men to fulfill their potential. Educated women are more likely to challenge discriminatory practices and advocate for gender equality in all spheres of life, from politics and economics to culture and social norms. Through education, women become agents of social change, driving progress towards a more just and equitable world.

5. Political Participation and Leadership: Educated women play a vital role in shaping democratic governance and political processes. When women are educated, they are more likely to participate in political activities, such as voting, running for office, and engaging in advocacy and activism. Increased female political participation leads to more representative and responsive governance, as women bring unique perspectives, priorities, and experiences to the decision-making table. Moreover, educated women are more likely to assume leadership roles in their communities and nations, serving as role models and mentors for future generations of women leaders.

6. Inter-generational Impact and Human Capital Development: Investing in women's education yields inter-generational benefits by influencing the health, education, and well-being of future generations. Educated women are more likely to invest in the education and health of their children, breaking the cycle of poverty and creating pathways to upward mobility. Furthermore, educated mothers play a crucial role in shaping the cognitive and socio-emotional development of their children, laying the foundation for their future success. By investing in women's education, societies can harness the multiplier effect of human capital development, leading to long-term improvements in social and economic outcomes.

7. Conflict Resolution and Peace-building: Educated women are essential agents of peace-building and conflict resolution in conflict-affected regions. Studies have shown that societies with higher levels of female education are more likely to experience peace and stability, as educated women contribute to the prevention and mitigation of conflicts through dialogue, negotiation, and community mobilization. Furthermore, educated women are more resilient in the face of violence and extremism, as they possess the knowledge and skills to challenge radical ideologies and promote tolerance, diversity, and coexistence.

8. Environmental Sustainability and Climate Resilience: Educating women is also essential for environmental sustainability and climate resilience. Educated women are more likely to adopt sustainable practices, such as family planning, sustainable agriculture, and natural resource management, which contribute to environmental conservation and mitigate the impacts of climate change. Moreover, educated women play a crucial role in raising awareness about environmental issues, advocating for policies and actions that promote sustainability, and mobilizing communities to take collective action to protect the planet for future generations.

9. Cultural and Social Development: Education fosters cultural and social development by promoting critical thinking, creativity, and cultural exchange. Educated women contribute to the enrichment of cultural heritage through their artistic expressions, literary works, and intellectual contributions. Furthermore, education enables women to engage in dialogue and collaboration across cultural and social divides, fostering mutual understanding, tolerance, and respect for diversity. By promoting education for women, societies can unlock their creative potential and harness the transformative power of culture for social cohesion and harmony.

In conclusion, the advantages of educating women are manifold and far-reaching, encompassing empowerment, economic development, health, gender equality, political participation, inter-generational impact, conflict resolution, environmental sustainability, and cultural development. By investing in women's education, societies can unlock the full potential of women as agents of change and progress, leading to more prosperous, equitable, and sustainable futures for all. As we strive towards the realization of the Sustainable Development Goals, prioritizing women's education must remain a central pillar of our efforts to build a better world for present and future generations.

1. 6 - Problems Related to Women Education

Despite the recognized importance of women's education in fostering empowerment, promoting gender equality, and driving socio-economic development, numerous challenges persist that hinder women's access to education and their ability to fully benefit from it. These challenges are multifaceted and encompass a range of socio-cultural, economic, and structural barriers that disproportionately affect women and girls around the world. Understanding and addressing these problems is essential for advancing gender equality and ensuring that all women have equal opportunities to access quality education and realize their full potential.

1. Socio-Cultural Barriers: Socio-cultural norms and attitudes often serve as significant barriers to women's education, perpetuating traditional gender roles and stereotypes that prioritize boys' education over girls'. In many societies, girls are expected to prioritize household chores and caregiving responsibilities over education, leading to lower school enrollment and higher dropout rates among girls compared to boys. Moreover, harmful practices such as child marriage, gender-based violence, and female genital mutilation further inhibit girls' access to education and perpetuate cycles of poverty and inequality.

2. Economic Constraints: Economic factors play a crucial role in limiting women's access to education. Poverty is a significant barrier that prevents many families from sending their daughters to school, as they may prioritize limited resources for their sons' education or household expenses. Additionally, indirect costs such as school fees, uniforms, books, and transportation often pose insurmountable financial burdens for families, particularly in low-income and marginalized communities. As a result, girls from impoverished backgrounds are disproportionately affected by educational exclusion and are more likely to be denied the opportunity to pursue their educational aspirations.

3. Gender-Based Discrimination: Gender-based discrimination within educational institutions and systems remains a pervasive problem that undermines women's educational rights and opportunities. Girls often face systemic barriers such as discriminatory admissions policies, unequal access to resources and facilities, and gender-based violence in schools, which create hostile learning environments and discourage girls from attending or staying in school. Moreover, entrenched biases and stereotypes among teachers and administrators can contribute to lower expectations for girls' academic achievement and limit their educational and career aspirations.

4. Lack of Accessible Infrastructure: Inadequate infrastructure and facilities pose significant challenges to women's education, particularly in rural and remote areas where schools may be inaccessible or poorly equipped. Many communities lack basic amenities such as safe and sanitary school buildings, clean water and sanitation facilities, and adequate transportation networks, which can deter girls from attending school, particularly during menstruation. Additionally, the absence of female teachers and gender-sensitive educational materials further exacerbates the barriers to girls' education, as they may lack role models and face difficulties accessing relevant and culturally appropriate learning resources.

5. Early Marriage and Pregnancy: Early marriage and pregnancy remain major impediments to girls' education in many parts of the world. Girls who are married off at a young age are often forced to drop out of school to fulfill traditional gender roles as wives and mothers, denying them the opportunity to complete their education and pursue their aspirations. Moreover, early pregnancy can have detrimental effects on girls' health, well-being, and educational attainment, as they may face stigma, discrimination, and limited support to continue their studies while managing the responsibilities of motherhood.

6. Lack of Quality Education: Even when girls have access to schooling, the quality of education they receive may be substandard, perpetuating inequalities and limiting their opportunities for learning and advancement. Many schools lack trained and qualified teachers, particularly in rural and marginalized communities, which can result in inadequate instruction and low academic achievement levels. Additionally, curricula may be outdated, irrelevant, or gender-biased, reinforcing stereotypes and limiting girls' exposure to diverse perspectives and knowledge domains. Furthermore, schools may lack adequate resources, such as textbooks, teaching materials, and technology, further compromising the quality of education provided to girls.

7. Cultural and Social Norms: Cultural and social norms often dictate gender roles and expectations, shaping individuals' attitudes and behaviors towards women's education. In many communities, prevailing beliefs about gender and education prioritize boys' schooling over girls', perpetuating cycles of inequality and discrimination. Moreover, societal perceptions of girls' intellectual abilities and educational potential may be influenced by stereotypes and biases, leading to lower expectations for girls' academic achievement and limiting their opportunities for educational advancement. Addressing these cultural and social norms requires comprehensive efforts to challenge stereotypes, promote gender equality, and empower communities to support girls' education.

8. Conflict and Humanitarian Crises: Conflict, displacement, and humanitarian crises pose significant challenges to women's education, disrupting educational systems and exacerbating existing barriers to access and retention. During conflicts, schools may be destroyed or occupied by armed forces, depriving girls of safe and conducive learning environments. Additionally, displacement and instability may force families to prioritize immediate survival needs over education, leading to increased dropout rates and educational disruption. Moreover, girls in conflict-affected areas are at heightened risk of gender-based violence, including sexual exploitation, trafficking, and forced recruitment, further undermining their access to education and well-being.

9. Limited Opportunities for Higher Education and Skills Development: Even when girls overcome barriers to access basic education, they may face limited opportunities for higher education and skills development, particularly in fields traditionally dominated by men. Higher education institutions may have limited capacity to accommodate female students, or they may lack programs and resources that are relevant and accessible to women. Additionally, cultural and societal expectations may discourage girls from pursuing higher education or entering non-traditional fields, limiting their opportunities for economic empowerment and advancement.

10. Lack of Policy Support and Implementation: A lack of political will, policy support, and implementation mechanisms further undermines efforts to address the problems related to women's education. Many countries lack comprehensive and gender-responsive education policies that prioritize women's and girls' rights and address the systemic barriers to access and retention. Additionally, limited investment in education, particularly for marginalized populations, hinders efforts to improve infrastructure, quality, and accessibility. Without adequate policy support and implementation mechanisms, efforts to promote women's education are unlikely to achieve meaningful and sustainable impact.

In conclusion, the problems related to women's education are complex and interconnected, stemming from a combination of socio-cultural, economic, and structural factors. Addressing these challenges requires holistic and multi-dimensional approaches that prioritize gender equality, invest in quality education, and empower women and girls to overcome barriers and realize their full potential. By recognizing and addressing the root causes of educational exclusion and inequality, societies can unlock the transformative power of women's education and create more inclusive, equitable, and sustainable futures for all.

CHAPTER - 2

HISTORY OF WOMEN EDUCATION

Throughout history, the journey of women's education has been marked by struggles, milestones, and remarkable achievements. From ancient civilizations to the modern era, women have fought against societal norms, discrimination, and systemic barriers to access education and knowledge. Understanding the history of women's education illuminates the progress made, the challenges faced, and the ongoing efforts to achieve gender equality in education.

2. 1 - History of Women Education in Ancient India

During the Vedic period in ancient India, spanning from roughly 1500 BCE to 500 BCE, the status and role of women in society were significantly different from what would be observed in later historical periods. This era, often referred to as a golden age for women's education, saw women enjoying considerable freedom and opportunities for intellectual and spiritual development. The Vedic period is notable for its relatively egalitarian social structures, especially concerning education and intellectual pursuits. Women in the Vedic period were not only participants in household and social activities but also actively engaged in educational and scholarly endeavors.

The Rigveda, one of the oldest known texts, highlights the involvement of women in composing hymns and participating in scholarly debates. Women scholars were revered and respected for their wisdom, knowledge, and contributions to intellectual and spiritual life. Prominent among these scholars were Gargi and Maitreyi, whose contributions have been documented in ancient texts. Gargi Vachaknavi was a renowned philosopher who is particularly famous for her participation in the philosophical debates recorded in the Upanishads. In the Brihadaranyaka Upanishad, Gargi is depicted engaging in a profound debate with the sage Yajnavalkya, challenging him on complex metaphysical concepts. Her questions and arguments were not only indicative of her deep understanding but also demonstrated the high regard in which women's intellectual capabilities were held during this period.

Similarly, Maitreyi, another esteemed woman scholar of the Vedic period, was a philosopher and the wife of sage Yajnavalkya. She is well-known for her significant contributions to spiritual and philosophical discourse, particularly in her dialogues with Yajnavalkya, where she expressed deep interest in understanding the nature of the self and the pursuit of knowledge. Maitreyi's dialogues are notable for their emphasis on the impermanence of material wealth and the importance of spiritual wisdom, reflecting the intellectual rigor and philosophical inquiry encouraged during this era. The educational system in the Vedic period, particularly the Gurukul system, played a crucial role in the dissemination of knowledge. In the Gurukul system, students lived with their teachers (gurus) and received education through direct instruction and practical experience.

This system was inclusive, allowing women to study alongside men. Education for women was not confined to the upper classes; it extended to various social strata, enabling a broader segment of society to benefit from learning and intellectual growth. Women were educated in a wide range of subjects, including the Vedas, philosophy, astronomy, medicine, and other branches of knowledge. The Vedas, the foundational scriptures of Hinduism, were central to the educational curriculum. Women who studied the Vedas were known as Brahmavadinis. They were not only knowledgeable in religious texts but also proficient in reciting and interpreting these scriptures. The respect accorded to these women scholars underscores the inclusive and progressive nature of Vedic society regarding education and intellectual pursuits.

In addition to the Vedas, women in the Vedic period had access to education in various other fields. For instance, the study of philosophy allowed them to engage in intellectual debates and explore profound questions about existence, ethics, and the nature of the universe. Astronomy and medicine were also part of the curriculum, enabling women to contribute to scientific and medical knowledge. The holistic approach to education in the Vedic period aimed at the overall intellectual and spiritual development of individuals, irrespective of gender. The participation of women in intellectual and religious activities was not merely symbolic but substantive. Women were actively involved in performing religious rituals, composing hymns, and participating in scholarly debates. The Rigveda mentions several women rishis (sages) who composed hymns and were considered seers of divine knowledge. Their contributions were integral to the spiritual and intellectual fabric of Vedic society.

Moreover, the Vedic period was characterized by a relatively egalitarian approach to gender roles, particularly in the context of education. The intellectual and spiritual development of both men and women was encouraged, fostering a culture of learning and growth. This inclusive environment allowed women to attain high levels of scholarship and contribute meaningfully to various fields of knowledge. The respect and opportunities afforded to women in the Vedic period contrast sharply with the later periods of Indian history, where women's roles became more restricted due to socio-political changes and the influence of patriarchal structures. The decline in the status of women and their access to education can be traced to the post-Vedic period, where societal norms and customs began to evolve in ways that limited women's freedoms and opportunities. Several factors contributed to the decline in women's status after the Vedic period.

The advent of foreign invasions, changes in socio-political structures, and the rise of patriarchal norms led to the marginalization of women in various spheres of life. The educational opportunities that were once widely accessible to women became restricted, and their roles were increasingly confined to domestic spheres. The shift from a relatively egalitarian society to a more hierarchical and patriarchal one resulted in the erosion of the freedoms and opportunities that women had enjoyed during the Vedic period. Despite these changes, the legacy of women's contributions during the Vedic period remained an important part of Indian cultural and intellectual history. The achievements of scholars like Gargi and Maitreyi continue to be celebrated and serve as a testament to the rich intellectual and spiritual traditions of ancient India. Their works and the educational practices of the Vedic period provide valuable insights into the progressive and inclusive nature of early Indian society.

In conclusion, the Vedic period in ancient India stands out as a remarkable era for women's education and intellectual participation. Women enjoyed considerable freedom and were actively involved in various fields of knowledge, contributing significantly to intellectual and spiritual life. The inclusive and egalitarian approach to education during this period fostered a culture of learning and growth, allowing women to attain high levels of scholarship and respect. The contributions of women scholars like Gargi and Maitreyi highlight the high regard for women's intellectual capabilities and the progressive nature of Vedic society. While the status of women declined in later periods, the legacy of their contributions during the Vedic period continues to be an important part of India's cultural and intellectual heritage.

The post-Vedic period, spanning approximately from 500 BCE to the early centuries CE, witnessed a significant transformation in the social and cultural fabric of Indian society. This era marked a notable decline in the status and rights of women, particularly concerning education and intellectual participation. Several factors, including the rise of patriarchal norms, socio-political changes, and economic transformations, contributed to this regression. The transition from a relatively egalitarian society during the Vedic period to a more patriarchal one had profound implications for women's educational opportunities and their roles in society. One of the primary reasons for the decline in women's status during the post-Vedic period was the strengthening of patriarchal structures. The emphasis on male dominance in both the family and society became more pronounced, leading to the marginalization of women. Patriarchal norms dictated that women's primary roles were those of wives and mothers, responsible for maintaining the household and raising children.

This societal shift relegated women to domestic spheres, severely limiting their participation in public life and education. The rise of patriarchal structures was closely tied to changes in socio-economic conditions. As societies became more agrarian and feudal, the importance of land ownership and inheritance increased. Protecting family honor and lineage became paramount, leading to stricter controls over women's behavior and mobility. These controls often manifested in practices such as child marriage, seclusion of women (purdah), and the restriction of women's education to preserve family honor and ensure their chastity. The focus on family honor and lineage often resulted in early marriages, where young girls were married off before they had the opportunity to pursue education. Religious and legal texts from the post-Vedic period also played a significant role in shaping societal attitudes towards women.

The Manusmriti, one of the most influential legal texts of ancient India, codified many of the patriarchal norms and practices that marginalized women. According to the Manusmriti, women were to be under the guardianship of their fathers, husbands, and sons at different stages of their lives, effectively denying them autonomy and independence. The text emphasized women's roles as dutiful wives and mothers, further reinforcing the notion that their primary responsibilities lay within the domestic sphere. These religious and legal prescriptions had a profound impact on women's educational opportunities. Formal education for women became increasingly rare, as societal norms dictated that women should focus on household duties. The decline in women's education was also reflected in the reduction of female scholars and intellectuals during this period.

Unlike the Vedic period, which celebrated women like Gargi and Maitreyi for their intellectual contributions, the post-Vedic period saw fewer examples of women engaging in scholarly pursuits. The decline in women's educational opportunities was not uniform across all regions and communities. Some regions and communities continued to value women's education to varying degrees. For instance, certain Buddhist and Jain monastic communities provided educational opportunities for women, allowing them to become nuns and pursue spiritual and intellectual growth. However, these instances were exceptions rather than the norm, and the overall trend was towards a reduction in educational access for women. The impact of these societal changes on women's education was multifaceted. Firstly, the restriction of women's mobility and the emphasis on domestic roles meant that fewer women had the opportunity to attend educational institutions or study under teachers.

The Gurukul system, which had been inclusive during the Vedic period, became less accessible to women as societal norms discouraged their participation. Secondly, the focus on protecting family honor often led to the seclusion of women, further isolating them from educational and intellectual pursuits. Practices such as purdah, where women were kept in seclusion from men outside their immediate family, became more prevalent, limiting their interactions with the broader society and restricting their access to education. Moreover, the shift in societal attitudes towards women's education had long-term implications for their roles in society. As educational opportunities diminished, women were increasingly confined to roles that required little formal education. This confinement to domestic duties not only limited their personal growth and development but also curtailed their contributions to broader societal and intellectual discourses.

The loss of educational opportunities meant that women were less able to participate in decision-making processes, both within the household and in the wider community. Despite the overall decline in women's educational opportunities during the post-Vedic period, there were some noteworthy exceptions and efforts to counteract these trends. For instance, certain royal courts and families continued to educate their daughters, recognizing the value of an educated woman in maintaining cultural and intellectual traditions. Women from royal and noble families occasionally received instruction in subjects such as literature, music, and the arts, though these opportunities were limited compared to those available to men. Additionally, the rise of various religious movements during the post-Vedic period provided alternative avenues for women's education and spiritual growth.

The Bhakti movement, which emerged around the 7th century CE, emphasized personal devotion to a deity and rejected rigid caste and gender distinctions. This movement allowed women to participate more actively in religious and devotional practices, creating spaces where they could express their spirituality and, in some cases, engage in intellectual discourse. Women saints and poets such as Andal, Akka Mahadevi, and Mirabai became prominent figures in the Bhakti movement, using their poetry and songs to express their devotion and challenge societal norms. Similarly, the rise of Jainism and Buddhism provided some women with opportunities to pursue education and spiritual growth. Buddhist monasteries, in particular, offered women the chance to become nuns and engage in religious study and practice. The establishment of nunneries allowed women to pursue education and spiritual development outside the constraints of traditional household roles. However, these opportunities were still relatively limited compared to the widespread educational access women enjoyed during the Vedic period.

In summary, the post-Vedic period marked a significant decline in the status and educational opportunities of women in India. The rise of patriarchal norms, coupled with socio-economic changes and the influence of religious and legal texts, contributed to the marginalization of women in educational and public spheres.

Women's roles became more confined to domestic duties, and their opportunities for formal education were significantly reduced. The decline in women's educational status during the post-Vedic period was also influenced by religious and cultural texts that began to emphasize women's roles as wives and mothers. The Manusmriti, a legal text from ancient India, codified gender roles and prescribed duties for women that primarily centered around household responsibilities. These texts reinforced the notion that a woman's primary duty was to her family, thereby limiting her educational and professional aspirations. As a result, the intellectual pursuits that women engaged in during the Vedic period became less accessible, and women's contributions to scholarly and public life diminished.

2. 2 - History of Women Education in Medieval India

The medieval period in India, roughly spanning from the 6th to the 18th century, saw a further decline in the status and educational opportunities for women. This era was characterized by the establishment of various kingdoms and empires, the consolidation of patriarchal norms, and the advent of foreign invasions.

These factors collectively contributed to the marginalization of women and the restriction of their educational and public roles. The societal and cultural dynamics of this period created an environment where women's access to education was severely limited, and their participation in public life was greatly curtailed. The establishment of various kingdoms and empires during the medieval period often led to the reinforcement of patriarchal norms and customs. As these political entities sought to consolidate their power and maintain social order, they increasingly relied on patriarchal structures to regulate family and community life. The emphasis on protecting family honor and lineage became more pronounced, leading to stricter controls over women's behavior, mobility, and educational opportunities. This period saw the widespread adoption of practices such as purdah (seclusion) and child marriage, which further restricted women's access to education.

The advent of foreign invasions, particularly by the Turks and Mughals, introduced new cultural influences that had a profound impact on Indian society. These invasions often brought with them different social and cultural practices that further curtailed women's freedoms. The practice of purdah, for example, became more widespread as a result of these cultural exchanges. Purdah involved the seclusion of women from public view, restricting their movements and interactions with the broader society. This practice not only limited women's ability to pursue education but also isolated them from participating in public life and intellectual discourse. Child marriage became another prevalent practice during the medieval period. Girls were often married off at a very young age, which effectively ended their educational pursuits before they could even begin. The focus on early marriage was driven by concerns over protecting family honor and ensuring the chastity of young women.

Once married, women's roles were largely confined to domestic duties, and their opportunities for formal education were significantly reduced. The early age at which girls were married meant that their potential for intellectual and personal development was stifled, reinforcing their dependence on their husbands and families. Educational opportunities for women during the medieval period were largely confined to the elite classes. Royal women and those from affluent families sometimes received education, but even then, it was limited in scope and conducted in seclusion. These women might have been educated in subjects such as literature, music, and fine arts, but their studies were often carried out within the confines of the palace or household. The education they received was not intended to prepare them for public roles but rather to enhance their abilities to manage household affairs and entertain guests.

For the general population of women, access to formal education was almost non-existent. Most women were engaged in agricultural or domestic labor, with little opportunity or encouragement to pursue education. The focus on domestic roles for women was reinforced by societal norms that valued their contributions to household management and child-rearing over intellectual pursuits. This lack of educational opportunities meant that the majority of women remained illiterate and were excluded from participating in the intellectual and cultural life of their communities. Despite these widespread restrictions, the medieval period also witnessed the emergence of the Bhakti and Sufi movements, which offered some respite for women's educational and spiritual pursuits. These movements emphasized personal devotion and spiritual equality, challenging the rigid caste and gender hierarchies of the time. The Bhakti movement, in particular, promoted a more inclusive approach to spirituality, allowing women to express their devotion and knowledge through poetry, music, and religious practices.

Prominent women saints and poets, such as Andal, Akka Mahadevi, and Mirabai, emerged from the Bhakti movement. These women used their poetry and songs to express their deep devotion to God and to challenge societal norms that restricted women's roles. Mirabai, for example, defied the expectations of her royal background by becoming a wandering devotee and poet, singing about her love for Lord Krishna and rejecting the constraints imposed on her by society. Her works and life story inspired many and demonstrated that women could transcend societal limitations through spiritual devotion. Similarly, the Sufi movement within Islam promoted a more inclusive spiritual practice that welcomed women's participation. Sufi mystics emphasized the direct and personal experience of God, often through poetry and music, and allowed women to join their spiritual gatherings and express their devotion.

Women like Rabia Basri became renowned for their spiritual insights and contributions to Sufi literature. These movements, while offering some opportunities for women's intellectual and spiritual growth, were exceptions rather than the norm and did not significantly alter the overall educational landscape for women during the medieval period. The educational institutions that did exist during the medieval period, such as madrasas and pathshalas, were primarily oriented towards male students. Madrasas, which were centers of Islamic learning, focused on religious education, jurisprudence, and sciences, but they were generally not accessible to women. Pathshalas, traditional Hindu schools, also catered predominantly to boys, providing instruction in religious texts, languages, and basic arithmetic. The exclusion of women from these educational institutions further entrenched their marginalization and limited their opportunities for intellectual development.

In some regions, however, there were occasional efforts to educate women. Certain royal courts and noble families recognized the value of an educated woman in maintaining cultural and intellectual traditions. Women in these contexts might receive instruction in subjects such as literature, music, and the arts, albeit within the confines of their homes or palaces. These instances were rare and typically confined to the upper echelons of society, where women had the resources and support to pursue limited forms of education. The broader cultural and intellectual climate of the medieval period also played a role in shaping attitudes towards women's education. The period saw significant developments in literature, philosophy, and the arts, but these fields were dominated by male scholars and practitioners. Women's contributions were often overlooked or undervalued, and their participation was largely limited to the private sphere.

The male-centric nature of intellectual life meant that women's voices and perspectives were rarely included in the broader cultural discourse. Despite the numerous challenges and restrictions, some women managed to make significant contributions to literature, arts, and spirituality during the medieval period. Their achievements stand as testament to their resilience and determination in the face of societal limitations. These women, though few in number, demonstrated that education and intellectual pursuits were not entirely out of reach, even in a highly restrictive environment. In conclusion, the medieval period in India saw a marked decline in women's educational status and opportunities. The consolidation of patriarchal norms, the impact of foreign invasions, and the widespread adoption of practices such as purdah and child marriage severely restricted women's access to education and their participation in public life.

Educational opportunities were largely confined to elite women, and even then, they were limited and conducted in seclusion. The Bhakti and Sufi movements provided some respite, promoting more inclusive spiritual practices and allowing women to express their devotion and knowledge. However, these movements were exceptions rather than the norm, and the overall educational landscape for women remained bleak. Despite these challenges, the resilience and contributions of women during this period highlight their determination to pursue intellectual and spiritual growth in the face of significant societal limitations. The medieval period's complex and evolving nature of women's roles and status reflects the broader historical trends that shaped Indian society and culture.

2. 3 - History of Women Education in Modern India

The trajectory of women's education in India took a significant turn during the modern period, marked by the advent of British colonial rule in the 18th century, and continuing through India's independence in 1947 and into the present day. This era has been characterized by profound social, political, and economic changes, leading to substantial improvements in women's educational status and opportunities. The journey towards gender equality in education, however, has been complex and multifaceted, influenced by various social reform movements, legislative changes, and ongoing efforts to address systemic barriers.

The British colonial period in India, spanning from the mid-18th century to the mid-20th century, marked a significant transformation in the Indian education system. The traditional, largely informal and community-based education system began to be replaced by a more formal, Western-style system. While the primary focus of this new system was on educating boys, it also inadvertently laid the groundwork for reforms in women's education.

2. 3. 1 - Early Colonial Education and Women

When the British East India Company established control over large parts of India, one of their key objectives was to create an administrative machinery that could effectively manage their territories. This necessitated the creation of an educated class of Indians who could assist in the administration. The early colonial education efforts were primarily aimed at boys from affluent families who could be trained to serve in subordinate roles within the colonial administration. However, the introduction of Western education also brought new ideas and social values, which gradually began to influence Indian society. The British educational policies, although not initially focused on women, created an environment where the need for educating women began to be recognized. The establishment of schools, colleges, and universities following a structured curriculum started to challenge the deeply entrenched patriarchal norms that restricted women's access to education.

Social Reformers and Advocacy for Women's Education

The colonial period saw the emergence of several Indian social reformers who played pivotal roles in advocating for women's education. These reformers recognized the intrinsic value of educating women and worked tirelessly to promote educational opportunities for them.

1. **Raja Ram Mohan Roy-** One of the most notable reformers of the time, Raja Ram Mohan Roy, campaigned against social evils like Sati (the practice of widow immolation) and supported the cause of women's education. He believed that education was essential for women's empowerment and societal progress. Roy's efforts led to the abolition of Sati in 1829, creating a more conducive environment for advocating women's rights, including education.

2. **Ishwar Chandra Vidyasagar-** Another prominent reformer,

Ishwar Chandra Vidyasagar, was instrumental in promoting widow remarriage and women's education. Vidyasagar's deep concern for the plight of women, particularly widows, drove him to open several schools for girls in Bengal. He believed that education was the key to social reform and worked to provide educational opportunities for women, despite facing significant opposition from conservative elements in society.

3. **Jyotirao Phule and Savitribai Phule-** Perhaps the most revolutionary figures in the field of women's education during the colonial period were Jyotirao Phule and his wife Savitribai Phule. In 1848, they established the first girls' school in Pune, a landmark event in the history of women's education in India. Savitribai Phule, often regarded as India's first female teacher, played a crucial role in this endeavor. Despite facing severe backlash, including social ostracism and physical threats, the Phules remained steadfast in their commitment to educating girls and challenging caste and gender discrimination.

Institutional Support and Government Initiatives

The British colonial government, though primarily focused on establishing an education system for administrative purposes, began to recognize the importance of women's education as social reforms gained momentum. This recognition was partly driven by the efforts of Indian reformers and partly by the British administrators who saw the need for social development as part of their civilizing mission.

First Women's College- In 1871, the colonial government supported the establishment of Bethune College in Kolkata, the first women's college in India. This institution marked a significant step forward in providing formal higher education to women. Bethune College offered a curriculum that included literature, science, and other subjects, paving the way for women's participation in higher education.

1. **Missionary Contributions** Christian missionaries also played a vital role in advancing women's education during the

colonial period. Missionary schools for girls were established in various parts of the country, often focusing on basic literacy, religious education, and vocational training. While the primary motive of these missionary schools was to convert Indian women to Christianity, they nonetheless contributed to the broader movement of women's education.

2. **Resistance and Challenges:** Despite these advancements, the movement for women's education faced considerable resistance from conservative factions within Indian society. Patriarchal norms, deep-rooted caste prejudices, and fear of social change created significant barriers. Many families were reluctant to send their daughters to school, fearing that education would make them less marriageable or lead them to question traditional gender roles. Moreover, the British colonial policies were not entirely altruistic and were often limited in scope. The focus remained primarily on creating a class of educated men who could assist in the administration. Women's education, while gaining support, was not prioritized at the same level as men's education.

3. **The Legacy of Reformers:** The relentless efforts of social reformers during the colonial period laid the foundation for the future progress of women's education in India. The schools and colleges established during this time, although limited in number and scope, provided a model that could be expanded upon in the post-independence era. The contributions of reformers like Raja Ram Mohan Roy, Ishwar Chandra Vidyasagar, and Jyotirao Phule created a legacy of advocacy for women's rights and education that continued to inspire subsequent generations. Their work highlighted the critical link between education and social reform, demonstrating that empowering women through education was essential for the overall progress of society.

4. **Post-Independence Developments:** The seeds of reform sown during the colonial period bore fruit in the post-independence era. After gaining independence in 1947, India's new government

made significant efforts to expand educational opportunities for women.

The Constitution of India, adopted in 1950, guaranteed the right to education for all citizens, irrespective of gender. Government policies and programs were introduced to promote universal education, reduce gender disparities, and improve access to education for girls. Initiatives like the National Policy on Education, the establishment of the University Grants Commission, and various scholarship programs for girls reflected the commitment to achieving gender equality in education.

5. **Continuing the Journey:** The colonial period, despite its many complexities and challenges, marked the beginning of a transformative journey for women's education in India. The efforts of social reformers, coupled with the gradual support from the colonial government, initiated a process of change that would continue to evolve in the following decades. Today, India has made significant strides in women's education, with increasing literacy rates, higher enrollment in schools and colleges, and growing representation of women in various professional fields. However, the journey is far from complete, and ongoing efforts are needed to address the persistent barriers and ensure that all women in India have access to quality education. The seeds of reform planted during the colonial period have grown into a movement that continues to push for greater equality and empowerment for women through education. As India moves forward, the legacy of these early reformers serves as a reminder of the transformative power of education and the importance of continuing the fight for gender equality.

2. 3. 2 - Colonial Period

The British colonial period in India marked the beginning of a renewed focus on women's education, driven by social reformers and missionaries. During the 19th century, several Indian reformers recognized the importance of educating women and advocated for their rights. Raja Ram Mohan Roy, a prominent social reformer, was a vocal advocate for women's education and played a key role in abolishing practices like Sati (the immolation of widows). He, along with other reformers like Ishwar Chandra Vidyasagar, emphasized the need for women's education to improve their social status and empower them to contribute to society.

Ishwar Chandra Vidyasagar, in particular, was instrumental in promoting women's education in Bengal. He established several schools for girls and worked tirelessly to change societal attitudes towards female education. Vidyasagar's efforts led to the establishment of the first schools for girls, which laid the foundation for women's formal education in India. The British colonial administration also supported these initiatives to some extent, recognizing the need for social reform and the role of education in achieving it. Christian missionaries played a significant role in promoting women's education during the colonial period. They established numerous schools and colleges for girls, providing them with access to modern education. Institutions like Bethune College in Kolkata, founded in 1879, were among the first women's colleges in India and set a precedent for higher education for women.

These missionary efforts, combined with the work of Indian reformers, led to a gradual increase in female literacy rates and educational opportunities. Social reform movements such as the Brahmo Samaj, Arya Samaj, and Prarthana Samaj also contributed significantly to the cause of women's education. Leaders like Jyotirao Phule and his wife Savitribai Phule, who opened the first school for girls in Pune in 1848, were at the forefront of these efforts. Savitribai Phule, in particular, is remembered as one of India's first female teachers and a pioneer in women's education. The work of these reformers and movements helped challenge traditional norms and paved the way for greater acceptance of women's education.

2. 3. 3 - Post-Independence Era: Legislative and Institutional Framework

The period following India's independence in 1947 marked a new chapter in the pursuit of educational equality for women. The Indian Constitution, adopted in 1950, enshrined the principles of equality and non-discrimination, providing a strong legal foundation for promoting women's education. Article 15 prohibits discrimination on grounds of religion, race, caste, sex, or place of birth, and Article 21A guarantees the right to education for children aged 6 to 14 years. The government of independent India implemented various policies and programs aimed at improving access to education for all, including women. The establishment of the University Grants Commission (UGC) in 1956, the National Policy on Education (NPE) in 1968 and 1986, and the subsequent updates in 1992 and 2020, all emphasized the importance of women's education and sought to address gender disparities.

The mid-20th century saw the expansion of primary, secondary, and higher education institutions across the country. Special provisions were made to encourage the enrollment of girls, including the introduction of scholarships, free textbooks, and midday meal schemes. The implementation of the Sarva Shiksha Abhiyan (SSA) in 2001 aimed to universalize elementary education, with a particular focus on improving girls' enrollment and retention rates.

Progress and Challenges: Contemporary Landscape

In the contemporary period, India has made substantial progress in women's education. The literacy rate for women has significantly increased from 8. 86% in 1951 to 70. 3% in 2021. There has been a notable rise in the enrollment of girls at all levels of education, from primary to higher education. The government's initiatives, such as the Beti Bachao Beti Padhao (Save the Girl Child, Educate the Girl Child) campaign, launched in 2015, have further emphasized the importance of girls' education and gender equality.

Despite these advancements, several challenges persist in achieving full educational parity for women in India. Socio-economic barriers, cultural norms, and safety concerns continue to impede girls' education, particularly in rural and economically disadvantaged areas. Issues such as child marriage, gender-based violence, and inadequate sanitation facilities in schools disproportionately affect girls' ability to pursue education. Moreover, there are disparities in the quality of education and access to resources between urban and rural areas. While urban centers have better infrastructure and educational facilities, rural areas often lack the necessary resources, leading to lower enrollment and retention rates for girls.

Higher Education and Professional Fields

The participation of women in higher education has seen a remarkable increase in recent decades. Women are now pursuing higher education in diverse fields such as science, technology, engineering, and mathematics (STEM), as well as in the humanities, social sciences, and professional courses like medicine, law, and business administration. The establishment of women's universities, such as SNDT Women's University in Mumbai and Avinashilingam University for Women in Coimbatore, has provided additional opportunities for women's higher education. Furthermore, women have made significant strides in various professional fields. The increased presence of women in the workforce, including leadership roles in business, academia, politics, and civil services, reflects the positive impact of improved educational opportunities.

Prominent Indian women such as Kiran Mazumdar-Shaw (founder of Biocon), Indra Nooyi (former CEO of PepsiCo), and scientists like Tessy Thomas and Gagandeep Kang have become role models, inspiring younger generations of women to pursue their dreams and ambitions.

Government Initiatives and Policy Measures

The Indian government has continued to implement and update policies aimed at promoting women's education. The Right to Education (RTE) Act, enacted in 2009, mandates free and compulsory education for children aged 6 to 14 years, with a special focus on eliminating gender disparities. The National Education Policy (NEP) 2020 further emphasizes gender inclusion, aiming to ensure that all children, particularly girls, have access to quality education. The NEP 2020 also highlights the importance of vocational education and skill development, encouraging girls to pursue diverse career paths and become economically independent. Initiatives such as the National Scheme of Incentive to Girls for Secondary Education (NSIGSE) and the Kasturba Gandhi Balika Vidyalaya (KGBV) scheme aim to reduce dropout rates among girls and provide them with safe and supportive learning environments.

Non-Governmental Organizations and Community Efforts

In addition to government efforts, numerous non-governmental organizations (NGOs) and community-based initiatives have played a crucial role in advancing women's education in India. Organizations such as Pratham, Educate Girls, and the Nanhi Kali project have implemented programs to improve literacy rates, increase school enrollment, and support girls' education in marginalized communities. These organizations often work at the grassroots level, addressing specific barriers to education such as poverty, cultural norms, and infrastructure deficiencies. Their efforts include building schools, providing scholarships, conducting awareness campaigns, and involving local communities in promoting the value of girls' education.

Future Directions and Continued Advocacy

While significant progress has been made, the journey towards achieving full educational equality for women in India is ongoing. Continued advocacy and efforts are required to address the remaining challenges and ensure that all girls and women have access to quality education.

Future directions should include:

1. Enhancing Infrastructure- Improving school infrastructure, particularly in rural and remote areas, to provide safe and conducive learning environments for girls.

2. Addressing Socio-Economic Barriers- Implementing targeted interventions to support economically disadvantaged families and

reduce the financial burden of education on girls.

3. Promoting STEM Education- Encouraging girls to pursue education and careers in STEM fields through scholarships, mentorship programs, and awareness campaigns.

4. Combating Gender-Based Violence- Strengthening policies and measures to prevent and address gender-based violence in and around educational institutions.

5. Increasing Community Involvement- Engaging local communities in promoting the importance of girls' education and challenging cultural norms that hinder educational access.

6. Supporting Higher Education- Expanding opportunities for women in higher education and professional fields through scholarships, research grants, and institutional support.

In conclusion, the modern period in India has seen remarkable advancements in women's education, driven by legislative measures, government initiatives, and the efforts of social reformers and NGOs. While challenges remain, the continued commitment to promoting gender equality in education promises a brighter future for women in India, empowering them to contribute fully to the nation's social, economic, and cultural development. The progress made so far is a testament to the resilience and determination of countless individuals and organizations dedicated to the cause of women's education and empowerment.

2. 3. 4 - Post-Independence Period

With India's independence in 1947, the newly formed government prioritized education for all citizens, including women. The Indian Constitution, adopted in 1950, enshrined the right to education as a fundamental right and guaranteed equal opportunities for men and women. This commitment to education was reflected in various policies and programs aimed at promoting female literacy and ensuring gender parity in education. The National Policy on Education, first formulated in 1968 and revised in 1986 and 1992, emphasized the need to eliminate gender disparities in education. The policy called for special measures to encourage girls' education, including the provision of scholarships, free textbooks, and the establishment of schools and colleges for women. These efforts were further bolstered by programs like the Sarva Shiksha Abhiyan (SSA), launched in 2001, which aimed to achieve universal primary education and improve the quality of education for all children, with a special focus on girls.

Higher education opportunities for women also expanded significantly in the post-independence period. Universities and professional institutions opened their doors to female students, leading to a substantial increase in female enrollment in higher education. Women began to pursue careers in various fields, including medicine, engineering, law, and the sciences, breaking traditional barriers and contributing to the nation's development. Government initiatives like Beti Bachao, Beti Padhao (Save the Daughter, Educate the Daughter), launched in 2015, further emphasized the importance of girls' education. This campaign aimed to address the declining child sex ratio and promote the education and empowerment of girls across the country. By raising awareness and providing financial incentives, the campaign sought to ensure that girls received equal opportunities to succeed in education and beyond.

2. 3. 5 - Contemporary Period

Today, the landscape of women's education in India has undergone significant transformation. Women have greater access to education at all levels, from primary to tertiary education. Government policies and programs continue to focus on improving female literacy rates and ensuring gender parity in education. The introduction of digital education platforms and online learning resources has further expanded educational opportunities for women, especially in remote and underserved areas. Despite these advancements, challenges remain. Gender disparity in education persists, particularly in rural areas where socio-economic factors, cultural norms, and inadequate infrastructure can hinder girls' access to education. Dropout rates among girls remain a concern, often driven by early marriage, financial constraints, and safety issues.

Efforts to address these challenges include the construction of separate toilets for girls in schools, providing safe transportation, and implementing community awareness programs to change attitudes towards girls' education. Technological advancements have opened new avenues for women's education. Online learning platforms, digital classrooms, and e-learning resources have made education more accessible and flexible, allowing women to balance their studies with other responsibilities. Initiatives like Digital India aim to bridge the digital divide and ensure that women have access to the tools and resources needed for modern education. In conclusion, the history of women's education in India is a testament to the resilience and determination of social reformers and women themselves who fought for their right to learn and grow.

From the Vedic period, where women were revered as scholars, to the challenges of the post-Vedic and medieval periods, and the subsequent revival during the colonial and post-independence eras, women's education in India has seen significant evolution. Today, continuing efforts are needed to ensure that every girl and woman in India has access to quality education, enabling them to contribute fully to the nation's progress and development. The 19th century stands as a pivotal period in the history of women's education, witnessing significant advancements driven by social reform movements, evolving attitudes towards gender roles, and the burgeoning push for women's rights. This era marked a gradual shift in societal perceptions, recognizing the crucial importance of educating women not only for their personal development but also for their potential contributions to society at large.

The advancements in women's education during this period laid the foundation for greater gender equality and paved the way for the empowerment of women in various spheres of life. One of the key factors driving advancements in women's education during the 19th century was the rise of social reform movements advocating for improved access to education for all members of society, regardless of gender or social status. These movements, which emerged in response to the social and economic upheavals brought about by industrialization and urbanization, sought to address the inequalities and injustices prevalent in society. Central to their agenda was the promotion of education as a means of social upliftment and empowerment. In particular, the women's rights movement, which gained momentum throughout the 19th century, played a crucial role in advocating for women's access to education.

Leaders and activists such as Elizabeth Cady Stanton, Susan B. Anthony, and Lucretia Mott championed the cause of women's rights, including the right to education. They argued that denying women access to education not only perpetuated gender inequality but also hindered the progress and development of society as a whole. Furthermore, the 19th century witnessed a gradual shift in societal attitudes towards gender roles, with increasing recognition of women's intellectual capabilities and potential. Influential thinkers and writers of the time, such as Mary Wollstonecraft, advocated for the education of women, arguing that it was essential for their personal development and for the betterment of society. Wollstonecraft's seminal work, "A Vindication of the Rights of Woman, " published in 1792, called for equal educational opportunities for women, challenging the prevailing notion that women were inherently inferior to men.

As a result of these social and intellectual shifts, educational opportunities for women began to expand during the 19th century. While access to education remained limited for many women, particularly those from marginalized communities, progress was made in establishing schools and institutions specifically for the education of girls and young women. These institutions, which ranged from private academies to public schools and colleges, provided women with access to formal education and opportunities for intellectual and personal growth. One notable development in women's education during the 19th century was the establishment of women's colleges and universities. These institutions, founded by pioneering educators and philanthropists, offered women access to higher education and opportunities for academic and professional advancement.

One such institution was Mount Holyoke Female Seminary, founded in 1837 by Mary Lyon in Massachusetts, which became the first of the Seven Sisters colleges and set a precedent for women's education in the United States. The founding of women's colleges and universities represented a significant milestone in the history of women's education, providing women with access to higher learning and challenging the prevailing notion that women's intellectual pursuits were secondary to those of men. These institutions offered rigorous academic programs, fostering critical thinking, intellectual curiosity, and leadership skills among their students. They also provided women with opportunities to pursue careers in fields traditionally dominated by men, such as medicine, law, and academia. Moreover, the expansion of women's education during the 19th century was not limited to formal institutions of learning. Women's organizations and philanthropic societies played a crucial role in promoting educational opportunities for women and girls, particularly those from disadvantaged backgrounds.

These organizations, often led by prominent women activists and reformers, established scholarships, provided financial assistance, and lobbied for educational reforms to ensure that women had equal access to education. In addition to formal education, the 19th century also witnessed the emergence of alternative forms of education for women, including home schooling and self-directed learning. Many women, particularly those from rural or isolated communities, were unable to attend formal schools or colleges due to various constraints. In response, they sought out alternative avenues for education, often relying on self-study, correspondence courses, and community-based learning initiatives to further their intellectual and personal development. The advancements in women's education during the 19th century had profound implications for society as a whole, contributing to greater gender equality, social mobility, and economic empowerment.

Educated women were better equipped to participate in civic life, engage in political activism, and advocate for social change. They also had greater opportunities for economic independence and professional advancement, challenging traditional gender roles and reshaping the social and economic fabric of society. Furthermore, the achievements of women in the field of education during the 19th century paved the way for future generations of women to pursue their educational aspirations and make their mark on the world. The trailblazing efforts of women educators, activists, and reformers laid the foundation for the modern women's rights movement and inspired countless women to defy societal expectations and pursue their dreams.

In conclusion, the 19th century witnessed significant advancements in women's education, driven by social reform movements, changing attitudes towards gender roles, and the push for women's rights. The establishment of women's colleges and universities, the expansion of educational opportunities for women, and the emergence of alternative forms of education all contributed to greater gender equality and empowerment. The achievements of women educators, activists, and reformers during this period laid the foundation for the modern women's rights movement and inspired generations of women to pursue their educational aspirations and contribute to the advancement of society.

Context of Social Reform Movements

The 19th century was a time of profound social and economic change, marked by the industrial revolution and the rise of urbanization. These developments created new opportunities for women's employment outside the home, particularly in factories and mills. However, many women lacked the education and skills necessary to pursue these opportunities, prompting calls for educational reform to prepare them for roles in the workforce.

Advocacy for Women's Rights to Education

Figures like Mary Wollstonecraft in England and Elizabeth Cady Stanton in the United States emerged as prominent advocates for women's rights to education during the 19th century. Wollstonecraft's seminal work, "A Vindication of the Rights of Woman" (1792), challenged prevailing notions of female intellectual inferiority and argued passionately for women's access to education as a means of achieving equality with men. Similarly, Stanton, a leading figure in the American suffrage movement, advocated for women's rights to education and campaigned for the establishment of educational institutions for women.

Establishment of Women's Colleges and Seminaries

One of the most significant developments in women's education during the 19th century was the establishment of women's colleges and seminaries. These institutions provided avenues for higher education for women, offering courses in a variety of subjects, including literature, mathematics, history, and the sciences. While women's colleges initially faced challenges in terms of funding, resources, and curricular offerings compared to men's institutions, they played a crucial role in expanding educational opportunities for women and challenging traditional gender norms.

Challenges and Limitations

Despite the advancements made in women's education during the 19th century, significant challenges and limitations remained. Access to education remained uneven, particularly for women from marginalized communities and racial minorities who faced discrimination and barriers to entry. Moreover, the curriculum and pedagogy of women's education often reflected prevailing gender stereotypes and societal expectations, emphasizing domestic skills and moral education over intellectual pursuits.

Impact on Society

The advancements in women's education during the 19th century had a profound impact on society, paving the way for greater gender equality and social progress. Educated women began to enter professions traditionally dominated by men, including teaching, nursing, and social work, expanding their roles and opportunities in the public sphere. Moreover, the education of women contributed to broader social and cultural changes, challenging traditional notions of female inferiority and reshaping attitudes towards gender roles and women's rights.

Legacy and Lessons Learned

The 19th century witnessed significant strides in women's education, driven by the efforts of social reformers, educators, and women's rights advocates. The establishment of women's colleges and the advocacy for women's rights to education laid the groundwork for future advancements in women's rights and gender equality. However, the challenges and limitations faced by women in accessing education during this period serve as a reminder of the ongoing struggle for equal educational opportunities for all individuals, regardless of gender, race, or socio-economic status.

The 19th century was a transformative period in the history of women's education, marked by significant advancements driven by social reform movements and advocacy for women's rights. The establishment of women's colleges and the push for greater access to education for women laid the groundwork for future progress in women's rights and gender equality. While challenges and limitations remained, the efforts of educators, activists, and reformers during this period paved the way for greater opportunities and empowerment for women in the realm of education and beyond.

The history of women's education is a testament to the resilience, courage, and determination of women and girls to overcome barriers and pursue their right to education. From ancient civilizations to the modern era, women have challenged societal norms, fought for

CHAPTER - 3

CONTRIBUTION OF THINKERS FOR WOMEN EDUCATION

3. 1 - Raja Ram Mohan Roy

Raja Ram Mohan Roy, often hailed as the "Father of the Indian Renaissance, " was a visionary social reformer, philosopher, and advocate for women's rights and education in 19th-century India. His contributions to the empowerment of women and the promotion of their education were instrumental in challenging traditional norms and laying the groundwork for gender equality in Indian society.

Early Life and Background

Raja Ram Mohan Roy, a pivotal figure in the Indian Renaissance and the broader movements for social reform and modernization, was born on May 22, 1772, in Radhanagar, Bengal Presidency, British India, which is now located in the state of West Bengal, India. Born into a Brahmin family, he was exposed to the rich cultural and intellectual traditions of Hinduism from an early age. His family background and upbringing instilled in him a deep appreciation for learning and spiritual inquiry.

Roy's early life was marked by his immersion in traditional Hindu education. He received instruction in Sanskrit, the language of ancient Indian texts and scriptures, and delved into the study of Hindu philosophy, religious texts, and scriptures. His upbringing within the Brahminical tradition provided him with a solid foundation in classical Indian thought and culture, shaping his worldview and intellectual outlook in his formative years.

However, despite his traditional education, Roy's intellectual curiosity and thirst for knowledge led him to explore ideas beyond the confines of orthodox Hinduism. His exposure to Western ideas and philosophies through interactions with British colonial administrators and European scholars sparked his interest in social educational opportunities, and made significant contributions knowledge and scholarship. While progress has been made, ga remain in access to education, particularly for women fr marginalized communities and disadvantaged backgroun Achieving gender equality in education requires concerted efforts address systemic barriers, promote inclusive policies, and empow women and girls to realize their full potential through education. we look to the future, ensuring equal access to quality education all remains a critical goal in building a more just, equitable, prosperous world for generations to come.

reform and progressive thought. This encounter with Western ideas served as a catalyst for his subsequent intellectual journey and his advocacy for reforms in Indian society.

Roy's early exposure to Western ideas, particularly Enlightenment ideals of reason, rationality, and humanism, deeply influenced his thinking and worldview. He was drawn to the principles of individual liberty, equality before the law, and the pursuit of knowledge, which he saw as essential for the progress and modernization of Indian society. Inspired by the ideals of the Enlightenment, Roy sought to apply rational inquiry and critical thinking to the social, religious, and political issues of his time.

Roy's early experiences and intellectual awakening laid the groundwork for his subsequent career as a social reformer, thinker, and activist. His encounters with British colonial officials and European scholars broadened his horizons and exposed him to new ideas and perspectives, challenging his preconceived notions and beliefs. These experiences served as a catalyst for his advocacy for social reform and his commitment to the ideals of justice, equality, and human dignity.

Moreover, Roy's upbringing within the Brahminical tradition endowed him with a deep understanding of Hinduism and its philosophical underpinnings. However, he was also critical of certain aspects of Hindu society, particularly the caste system, religious orthodoxy, and superstition. Drawing upon his knowledge of Hindu scriptures and philosophy, Roy sought to reinterpret and reform Hinduism, emphasizing its universal and humanistic principles while challenging its dogmatic and discriminatory practices.

In addition to his intellectual pursuits, Roy's early life was marked by personal tragedies and challenges. The untimely death of his father during his childhood and the financial difficulties faced by his family forced him to confront adversity at a young age. These early hardships instilled in him a sense of resilience, determination, and empathy for the plight of the less fortunate, shaping his commitment to social justice and humanitarian causes.

Furthermore, Roy's early experiences of religious pluralism and cultural diversity in Bengal exposed him to different religious traditions and practices, fostering in him a spirit of tolerance, inclusivity, and religious ecumenism. He was deeply influenced by the teachings of Sufi mystics, Sikh gurus, and Christian missionaries, which emphasized the unity of all humankind and the importance of compassion, love, and service to others.

In conclusion, Raja Ram Mohan Roy's early life and background laid the foundation for his subsequent career as a pioneering social reformer, thinker, and activist. Born into a Brahmin family, he received a traditional education in Sanskrit and Hindu scriptures but was also exposed to Western ideas through interactions with British colonial administrators and European scholars. His intellectual curiosity, coupled with his exposure to diverse religious traditions and cultural influences, shaped his worldview and inspired his advocacy for social reform, religious tolerance, and human rights. Despite facing personal hardships and challenges, Roy's early experiences instilled in him a sense of resilience, empathy, and commitment to the welfare of society, which would define his life's work as a champion of justice, equality, and human dignity.

Advocacy for Women's Rights

Raja Ram Mohan Roy, widely regarded as the "Father of the Indian Renaissance, " was not only a pioneering social reformer and thinker but also a staunch advocate for women's rights in 19th-century India. Throughout his life, he vehemently opposed various social evils that oppressed women, including the practice of sati (widow burning), child marriage, and the purdah system (seclusion of women). Roy believed that these customs were not only morally reprehensible but also detrimental to the social and intellectual development of women, and he dedicated much of his life to campaigning for their abolition and advocating for gender equality.

One of the most significant causes that Roy championed was the abolition of sati, a practice in which widows were expected to immolate themselves on their husband's funeral pyres. Roy viewed sati as a barbaric custom that violated the fundamental rights of women and went against the principles of justice, humanity, and compassion. As early as the 1810s, he began campaigning for the abolition of sati, arguing that it was not sanctioned by Hindu scriptures and was, in fact, a distortion of true Hindu teachings.

Roy's advocacy against sati was based on both moral and legal grounds. He argued that the practice was morally reprehensible and constituted a grave violation of women's rights and dignity. He also appealed to the principles of natural justice and human rights, asserting that no individual should be coerced or compelled to sacrifice their life against their will. Additionally, Roy challenged the prevailing notion that sati was an integral part of Hindu culture and tradition, contending that it was a social custom that had been misinterpreted and misused for centuries.

Moreover, Roy's campaign against sati was informed by his deep knowledge of Hindu scriptures and philosophy. He meticulously studied religious texts such as the Vedas, Upanishads, and Dharmashastras, and argued that none of these sacred texts endorsed or sanctioned the practice of sati. On the contrary, Roy contended that Hinduism upheld the principles of compassion, non-violence, and respect for life, and that sati was antithetical to these core values.

Roy's advocacy against sati gained momentum in the early 19th century, particularly after the passage of the Bengal Sati Regulation Act in 1829, which outlawed the practice in British India. Roy played a pivotal role in mobilizing public opinion and lobbying colonial authorities to enact legislation prohibiting sati. He wrote numerous pamphlets, articles, and petitions denouncing the practice and calling for its abolition, garnering support from various quarters of society, including religious leaders, intellectuals, and social reformers.

In addition to his campaign against sati, Roy also advocated for the eradication of other harmful customs and practices that oppressed women, including child marriage and the purdah system. He recognized that these customs perpetuated the subjugation of women and hindered their social, economic, and intellectual advancement. Roy argued that child marriage deprived girls of their childhood and education, subjecting them to early motherhood and domestic servitude. Similarly, he condemned the purdah system, which confined women to the private sphere and denied them access to public life and opportunities for self-improvement.

Roy's advocacy for women's rights was not merely confined to theoretical discourse but also extended to practical initiatives aimed at empowering women and improving their social and economic status. He believed that education was the key to women's emancipation and actively promoted female education as a means of fostering independence, self-reliance, and empowerment. Roy supported the establishment of schools and educational institutions for girls, including the Hindu College in Calcutta, which admitted female students alongside male students.

Furthermore, Roy advocated for women's participation in public life and the professions, challenging traditional gender roles and stereotypes. He believed that women should have the same rights and opportunities as men to pursue their interests and aspirations, and he supported their involvement in fields such as journalism, literature, and social work. Roy's vision of gender equality encompassed not only legal and political rights but also social and economic empowerment, emphasizing the importance of women's autonomy and agency in all aspects of life.

Roy's advocacy for women's rights was ahead of its time and laid the groundwork for future generations of feminists and social reformers in India. His tireless efforts to challenge oppressive customs and promote gender equality inspired countless individuals to join the struggle for women's rights and paved the way for significant legislative reforms in the 19th and 20th centuries. Roy's legacy continues to resonate today as a testament to the power of ideas and activism in effecting positive change and advancing the cause of justice and equality for all.

Promotion of Women's Education

Raja Ram Mohan Roy, a towering figure in the Indian Renaissance and a pioneering advocate for social reform, made significant contributions to the promotion of women's education in 19th-century India. Recognizing the transformative power of education, Roy fervently advocated for the education of women, believing it to be essential for their empowerment and the advancement of society as a whole. He viewed education as a means of liberating women from ignorance and enabling them to fulfill their potential as active and engaged members of society. Roy's advocacy for women's education was rooted in his commitment to social justice, equality, and human dignity, and his efforts laid the foundation for the modern women's education movement in India.

From a young age, Roy was exposed to the importance of education and its potential to bring about social change. Growing up in Bengal during a time of political and intellectual ferment, he witnessed firsthand the impact of education on individuals and communities. Roy received a traditional education in Sanskrit and Hindu scriptures, but he also had the opportunity to engage with Western ideas and philosophies through interactions with British colonial administrators and European scholars. These experiences shaped his worldview and instilled in him a deep appreciation for the transformative power of education.

Roy's advocacy for women's education was motivated by a desire to uplift and empower women who were marginalized and oppressed by prevailing social norms and customs. He recognized that women's access to education was severely limited in traditional Indian society, where they were often confined to domestic roles and denied opportunities for intellectual and personal development. Roy believed that educating women was not only a matter of individual rights and dignity but also essential for the progress and prosperity of the nation as a whole.

One of Roy's central arguments in favor of women's education was the belief that educated women could play a vital role in shaping the future of society by raising educated and enlightened families. He argued that women were the primary educators of children and that their education was essential for instilling values of compassion, tolerance, and rational inquiry in future generations. Roy believed that educated mothers could create nurturing and supportive environments in which children could thrive intellectually, morally, and emotionally, thereby contributing to the overall well-being of society.

Furthermore, Roy believed that education was a fundamental human right that should be accessible to all individuals, regardless of gender or social status. He argued that denying women access to education was not only unjust but also detrimental to the progress and development of society as a whole. Roy firmly believed that women had the same inherent intellectual potential as men and that they deserved equal opportunities to acquire knowledge and skills that would enable them to lead fulfilling and meaningful lives.

In practical terms, Roy's advocacy for women's education encompassed various initiatives aimed at expanding educational opportunities for girls and young women. He supported the establishment of schools and educational institutions specifically for the education of girls, where they could receive instruction in a wide range of subjects, including languages, mathematics, science, and literature. Roy also advocated for the recruitment and training of female teachers to ensure that girls had access to quality education delivered by competent and dedicated educators.

Moreover, Roy believed that education should be holistic and comprehensive, addressing not only academic subjects but also moral and ethical values. He emphasized the importance of instilling in students a sense of social responsibility, civic engagement, and ethical conduct, which he believed were essential for creating a just and equitable society. Roy's vision of women's education was not merely focused on academic achievement but also on fostering character development and personal growth.

Roy's advocacy for women's education was not without its challenges and obstacles. He faced resistance from conservative elements within Indian society who opposed the idea of educating women and feared the social changes that education might bring about. Roy also encountered opposition from colonial authorities who were skeptical of his reformist agenda and wary of potential disruptions to the social order. Despite these challenges, Roy remained steadfast in his commitment to women's education and continued to advocate tirelessly for its promotion.

In conclusion, Raja Ram Mohan Roy's advocacy for women's education was rooted in his belief in the transformative power of education and its potential to bring about social change. He recognized that educating women was essential for their empowerment and the advancement of society as a whole. Roy's efforts laid the foundation for the modern women's education movement in India and inspired generations of educators, activists, and reformers to continue the struggle for gender equality and social justice. His legacy continues to resonate today as a testament to the enduring importance of education in the quest for human liberation and social progress.

Founding of the Hindu College

The founding of the Hindu College in Calcutta in 1817 marked a seminal moment in the history of education in India, particularly in the realm of higher education. At the forefront of this endeavor was Raja Ram Mohan Roy, a prominent social reformer and intellectual luminary of the time. Roy played a pivotal role in the establishment of the Hindu College, envisioning it as an institution that would provide modern, secular education to Indian youth, irrespective of gender or social background. His vision for the college went beyond mere academic pursuits; it aimed to foster critical thinking, intellectual inquiry, and moral character among its students, thereby laying the foundation for a progressive and enlightened society.

The Hindu College was founded against the backdrop of significant social and intellectual ferment in early 19th-century Bengal. The region was experiencing a period of cultural renaissance, characterized by a resurgence of interest in Indian literature, philosophy, and art, as well as a growing awareness of Western ideas and values. This intellectual awakening gave rise to a desire for educational reform and the establishment of institutions that would impart modern, scientific, and secular education to Indian youth.

Raja Ram Mohan Roy, a leading figure in the Indian Renaissance and a staunch advocate for social reform, recognized the importance of education as a catalyst for social change and national development. He believed that education had the power to liberate individuals from ignorance and superstition and to equip them with the knowledge and skills needed to navigate the complexities of the modern world. Inspired by the ideals of the Enlightenment and the progressive spirit of the times, Roy sought to establish educational institutions that would promote intellectual freedom, rational inquiry, and moral enlightenment.

The founding of the Hindu College was part of Roy's broader vision for educational reform in India. He envisioned the college as a center of learning that would provide students with a modern, liberal education grounded in the principles of reason, tolerance, and human dignity. Roy believed that education should be accessible to all members of society, regardless of their gender, caste, or social status, and he advocated for the inclusion of girls in the institution from its inception.

Roy's advocacy for the admission of girls to the Hindu College was revolutionary for its time. In early 19th-century India, access to education for girls was severely limited, and most educational institutions were exclusively reserved for boys. However, Roy recognized the importance of educating girls and argued that their inclusion in the college was essential for social reform and national progress. He believed that educated women would play a vital role in shaping the future of society by raising educated and enlightened families and contributing to the intellectual and cultural life of the nation.

Roy's efforts to promote the education of girls faced resistance from conservative elements within Indian society, who opposed the idea of educating women and feared the social changes that education might bring about. However, Roy remained steadfast in his commitment to women's education and continued to advocate tirelessly for the admission of girls to the Hindu College. His efforts eventually paid off, and in 1818, the college admitted its first female students, marking a significant milestone in the history of women's education in India.

The admission of girls to the Hindu College was met with enthusiasm and optimism by proponents of women's rights and educational reform. It was seen as a bold and progressive step towards gender equality and social justice, and it inspired other educational institutions to follow suit. In the years that followed, more colleges and schools began admitting female students, thereby expanding educational opportunities for girls and young women across the country.

The inclusion of girls in the Hindu College had far-reaching implications for Indian society. It challenged traditional gender roles and stereotypes, empowering women to pursue their educational aspirations and assert their rights as equal members of society. It also contributed to the broader movement for women's rights and social reform in India, inspiring generations of women to defy societal expectations and strive for equality and justice.

Moreover, the Hindu College played a significant role in shaping the intellectual and cultural landscape of Bengal and India as a whole. It attracted some of the brightest minds of the time, including scholars, poets, and social reformers, who engaged in lively debates and intellectual exchanges on a wide range of topics. The college became a hub of intellectual activity and social reform, fostering a spirit of critical inquiry, creativity, and social responsibility among its students.

In conclusion, the founding of the Hindu College in Calcutta in 1817 was a watershed moment in the history of education in India. Raja Ram Mohan Roy's visionary leadership and advocacy for the admission of girls to the institution marked a significant milestone in the advancement of women's education and gender equality in the country. The Hindu College paved the way for the establishment of other educational institutions that would provide modern, secular education to Indian youth, irrespective of their gender or social background. Its legacy continues to resonate today as a testament to the power of education to transform lives and societies for the better.

Promotion of Vernacular Education

Raja Ram Mohan Roy, a visionary social reformer and intellectual luminary of 19th-century India, was a staunch advocate for the promotion of vernacular education as a means of empowering the masses, including women. He recognized the pivotal role that education in the mother tongue played in making learning accessible to all segments of society, irrespective of their social or economic background. Roy firmly believed that education in vernacular languages was essential for enabling women, who were often marginalized and excluded from formal education, to participate more actively in social, cultural, and economic life and to challenge oppressive customs and traditions.

Roy's advocacy for vernacular education was grounded in his deep understanding of the socio-cultural dynamics of Indian society and his commitment to social justice and equality. He recognized that the majority of the population in India, particularly in rural areas, spoke vernacular languages such as Bengali, Hindi, and Urdu, and that providing education in these languages was crucial for ensuring widespread access to learning. Roy believed that education should be inclusive and accessible to all, regardless of their linguistic or cultural background, and he sought to promote vernacular education as a means of democratizing knowledge and empowering the masses.

One of Roy's most significant contributions to the promotion of vernacular education was his support for the establishment of schools and educational institutions that offered instruction in Bengali and other regional languages. He believed that providing education in the mother tongue would not only make learning more accessible to the masses but also foster a sense of pride and identity among students. Roy argued that education in vernacular languages would enable individuals to better understand and appreciate their cultural heritage and traditions, thereby strengthening their sense of belonging and connection to their communities.

Roy's advocacy for vernacular education was closely linked to his commitment to women's empowerment and gender equality. He recognized that women, who were often confined to domestic roles and denied access to formal education, stood to benefit significantly from education in their mother tongue. Roy believed that education was the key to liberating women from ignorance and superstition and enabling them to fulfill their potential as active and engaged members of society. By promoting vernacular education for women, Roy sought to empower them to challenge oppressive customs and traditions and to participate more fully in social, cultural, and economic life.

Furthermore, Roy saw vernacular education as a means of fostering social cohesion and national unity in a diverse and multicultural society like India. He believed that providing education in the mother tongue would help bridge linguistic and cultural divides and promote a sense of shared identity and belonging among different communities. Roy envisioned a pluralistic and inclusive society in which individuals from diverse linguistic and cultural backgrounds could coexist harmoniously and collaborate for the common good.

Roy's advocacy for vernacular education was not without its challenges and obstacles. He faced resistance from conservative elements within Indian society who viewed the promotion of vernacular languages as a threat to the dominance of Sanskrit and classical languages. Moreover, colonial authorities were skeptical of vernacular education and often favored English-medium schools as a means of promoting colonial interests and assimilating Indian elites into British culture. Despite these challenges, Roy remained steadfast in his commitment to vernacular education and continued to advocate tirelessly for its promotion.

One of the key strategies employed by Roy to promote vernacular education was the establishment of schools and educational institutions that offered instruction in Bengali and other regional languages. He supported the efforts of local communities and philanthropic organizations to set up schools that catered to the educational needs of children from diverse linguistic and cultural backgrounds. These schools provided basic literacy and numeracy skills, as well as instruction in subjects such as history, geography, and science, in the vernacular languages, thereby enabling students to acquire knowledge and skills that were relevant to their lives and communities.

Moreover, Roy advocated for the development of vernacular language textbooks and teaching materials that were culturally relevant and accessible to students from diverse backgrounds. He believed that educational materials should reflect the linguistic and cultural diversity of Indian society and that they should be designed in a way that appealed to students' interests and experiences. Roy also emphasized the importance of training and supporting teachers who were proficient in vernacular languages and who could effectively communicate with students and engage them in the learning process.

Roy's advocacy for vernacular education had a lasting impact on the educational landscape of India and contributed to the growth and development of regional languages and literatures. His efforts helped to establish a network of vernacular schools and educational institutions that provided basic education to millions of children, particularly in rural areas where access to formal education was limited. Roy's vision of vernacular education as a means of empowering the masses and promoting social justice and equality continues to inspire educators, policymakers, and social reformers in India and around the world.

Advocacy for Women's Rights in Education

Raja Ram Mohan Roy stands out in history as a formidable advocate for women's rights in education, championing the cause of equal educational opportunities for girls in 19th-century India. His advocacy was grounded in the belief that education was not only a fundamental human right but also the cornerstone of women's empowerment and social progress. Roy's tireless efforts to promote girls' education encompassed various initiatives aimed at establishing schools for girls, recruiting female teachers, and creating a conducive learning environment that would enable them to fulfill their potential and contribute to the betterment of society.

Roy's advocacy for women's rights in education was motivated by a deep sense of justice and equality. He recognized the systemic barriers that hindered girls' access to education in traditional Indian society and sought to challenge and dismantle these barriers through advocacy and activism. Roy believed that denying girls access to education was not only unjust but also detrimental to the progress and development of society as a whole. He argued that educated women could play a vital role in shaping the future of society by raising educated and enlightened families and contributing to the intellectual and cultural life of the nation.

One of Roy's most significant contributions to the promotion of women's rights in education was his advocacy for the establishment of schools for girls. He recognized that the lack of educational opportunities for girls was a significant impediment to their social and economic advancement and sought to address this issue by advocating for the establishment of schools specifically for girls. Roy believed that providing girls with access to education was essential for breaking the cycle of poverty and empowering them to lead fulfilling and meaningful lives.

Moreover, Roy campaigned for the recruitment of female teachers to provide girls with a conducive learning environment. He believed that female teachers could serve as role models and mentors for girls, inspiring them to pursue their educational aspirations and overcome obstacles. Roy recognized the importance of having female teachers who could understand and empathize with the unique challenges and experiences faced by girls and provide them with the support and encouragement they needed to succeed academically and personally.

Roy's advocacy for women's rights in education was rooted in his broader vision of social reform and progress. He believed that educating women was essential for challenging oppressive customs and traditions that perpetuated gender inequality and discrimination. Roy argued that education could empower women to assert their rights and advocate for their interests, thereby contributing to the creation of a more just, equitable, and inclusive society. He saw education as a powerful tool for transforming social attitudes and norms and promoting gender equality and social justice.

Furthermore, Roy recognized the interdependence between women's education and the overall development of society. He believed that investing in women's education was not only a moral imperative but also a sound economic investment that would yield significant social and economic dividends in the long run. Roy argued that educated women were more likely to participate in the labor force, contribute to household income, and invest in their children's education, thereby breaking the cycle of poverty and promoting sustainable development.

Roy's advocacy for women's rights in education was ahead of its time and laid the groundwork for future generations of feminists and social reformers in India. His tireless efforts to promote girls' education and gender equality inspired countless individuals to join the struggle for women's rights and paved the way for significant legislative reforms in the 19th and 20th centuries. Roy's legacy continues to resonate today as a testament to the enduring importance of education in the quest for gender equality and social justice.

In conclusion, Raja Ram Mohan Roy's advocacy for women's rights in education was driven by a deep commitment to justice, equality, and human dignity. He recognized the systemic barriers that hindered girls' access to education in traditional Indian society and sought to challenge and dismantle these barriers through advocacy and activism. Roy believed that educating women was not only a moral imperative but also essential for the progress and development of society as a whole. His tireless efforts to promote girls' education and gender equality laid the foundation for future generations of feminists and social reformers in India and around the world. Roy's legacy continues to inspire and empower individuals to advocate for women's rights and social justice in their communities and beyond.

Critique of Traditional Gender Roles

Raja Ram Mohan Roy was a trailblazing figure in challenging traditional gender roles and advocating for gender equality in 19th-century India. He recognized the inherent dignity and capabilities of women and vehemently opposed the societal norms that confined them to domestic duties and denied them access to education and employment opportunities. Roy's critique of traditional gender roles was rooted in his deep commitment to justice, equality, and human dignity, and his efforts paved the way for significant social and cultural transformations in Indian society.

Roy's critique of traditional gender roles was grounded in a profound understanding of the ways in which patriarchal norms and customs perpetuated gender inequality and discrimination. He observed how women were systematically excluded from the public sphere and relegated to subordinate roles within the family and community, denied the opportunity to pursue their aspirations and fulfill their potential. Roy saw this as a grave injustice and sought to challenge and dismantle the structures of oppression that denied women their rights and agency.

One of Roy's central arguments in his critique of traditional gender roles was the hypocrisy of a society that celebrated the virtues of women as mothers and wives but denied them the right to education and self-determination. He pointed out the contradiction inherent in praising women for their nurturing and caregiving roles while simultaneously denying them access to the tools and opportunities they needed to thrive as individuals. Roy argued that true respect for women required recognizing their inherent worth and allowing them the freedom to pursue their own interests and aspirations.

Roy's critique of traditional gender roles extended to the realm of education, where he saw the denial of educational opportunities to girls and women as a fundamental injustice. He believed that education was the key to empowering women and enabling them to challenge the social norms and expectations that confined them to subordinate roles. Roy argued that denying girls access to education not only deprived them of the opportunity to develop their talents and abilities but also perpetuated their dependence and subordination to men.

Moreover, Roy critiqued the traditional division of labor that assigned women to domestic duties and denied them the opportunity to participate fully in the economic and social life of society. He recognized that women's exclusion from the workforce and their dependence on men for economic support made them vulnerable to exploitation and abuse. Roy advocated for the economic independence of women and the recognition of their right to work and earn a livelihood, arguing that economic empowerment was essential for achieving gender equality and social justice.

Roy's critique of traditional gender roles was informed by his broader vision of social reform and progress. He believed that true progress could only be achieved by dismantling the structures of oppression and inequality that denied women their rights and freedoms. Roy saw gender equality as a prerequisite for a just and equitable society and worked tirelessly to challenge the patriarchal norms and customs that perpetuated gender discrimination and injustice.

Furthermore, Roy's critique of traditional gender roles was grounded in his commitment to religious and moral principles that emphasized the inherent dignity and equality of all human beings. He drew upon Hindu scriptures and philosophical traditions to argue for the equality of men and women and to challenge the hierarchical social order that placed men above women. Roy believed that true religious and moral values required treating women with respect and dignity and recognizing their rights as equal members of society.

In conclusion, Raja Ram Mohan Roy's critique of traditional gender roles was a powerful and influential force for social change in 19th-century India. He challenged the patriarchal norms and customs that confined women to subordinate roles and denied them access to education, employment, and self-determination. Roy's advocacy for gender equality was grounded in his deep commitment to justice, equality, and human dignity, and his efforts laid the foundation for significant social and cultural transformations in Indian society. His legacy continues to inspire and empower individuals to challenge gender inequality and work towards a more just and equitable world.

Legacy and Influence

Raja Ram Mohan Roy's legacy as a pioneering advocate for women's education and empowerment resonates strongly in India and beyond, leaving an indelible mark on the trajectory of social reform and feminist movements. His steadfast commitment to gender equality, justice, and human rights continues to inspire generations of activists, scholars, and policymakers as they strive to address persistent inequalities and empower women to realize their full potential.

Roy's advocacy for women's education was groundbreaking in its time, challenging prevailing norms and attitudes that relegated women to subordinate roles within society. His vision of education as a fundamental human right and a catalyst for social progress laid the groundwork for subsequent movements for women's rights and education in India. Roy's emphasis on the importance of educating women to promote their empowerment and participation in society remains a guiding principle for efforts to achieve gender equality and inclusive development.

Furthermore, Roy's advocacy for gender equality extended beyond the realm of education to encompass broader social and political issues. He was a vocal critic of discriminatory practices such as sati (widow burning) and child marriage, arguing that these customs violated basic human rights and hindered women's autonomy and agency. Roy's efforts to challenge these oppressive practices and promote women's rights paved the way for legal reforms and social change in India, setting a precedent for future generations of activists and reformers.

Roy's influence on the feminist movement in India cannot be overstated. His writings and speeches on women's rights and gender equality provided a theoretical foundation for feminist thought and activism in the country. Roy's insistence on the inherent equality and dignity of women challenged prevailing notions of female inferiority and subordination, inspiring generations of feminists to advocate for gender equality and social justice.

Moreover, Roy's advocacy for women's education and empowerment resonated with the broader principles of social reform and human rights that characterized the Indian Renaissance. His vision of a just and equitable society, where all individuals, regardless of gender, caste, or class, could live free from oppression and discrimination, inspired a new generation of social reformers to work towards the realization of this vision. Roy's legacy as a champion of women's rights and social justice continues to shape the feminist movement in India, providing a moral and intellectual compass for activists and advocates.

Roy's influence extends beyond India to the broader global context, where his ideas and principles have inspired movements for gender equality and human rights around the world. His advocacy for women's education as a means of empowerment resonates with efforts to promote girls' education and gender equality in developing countries. Roy's emphasis on the importance of challenging discriminatory practices and promoting women's rights as a fundamental aspect of human rights has informed international efforts to address gender-based violence, discrimination, and inequality.

Furthermore, Roy's advocacy for gender equality and social justice continues to inspire scholars and policymakers in their efforts to promote inclusive development and sustainable peace. His recognition of the interconnectedness of gender equality with broader social and economic development goals underscores the importance of mainstreaming gender perspectives in development policies and programs. Roy's legacy serves as a reminder of the enduring relevance of his ideas and principles in the pursuit of a more just, equitable, and inclusive world for all.

In conclusion, Raja Ram Mohan Roy's legacy as a pioneering advocate for women's education and empowerment continues to inspire social reformers, feminists, and human rights activists in India and around the world. His visionary leadership and steadfast commitment to gender equality, justice, and human rights laid the groundwork for subsequent movements for women's rights and education in India. Roy's ideas and principles remain as relevant today as they were in his time, providing a moral and intellectual foundation for efforts to achieve gender equality, social justice, and inclusive development.

Conclusion

In conclusion, Raja Ram Mohan Roy was a visionary social reformer whose advocacy for women's rights and education has left an indelible mark on Indian society. His efforts to challenge oppressive customs, promote women's education, and advance gender equality were ahead of his time and continue to resonate with contemporary struggles for women's empowerment. Raja Ram Mohan Roy's legacy serves as a reminder of the transformative power of education in empowering individuals and societies to create a more just and equitable world for all.

3. 2 - Maharshi Dhondo Keshav Karve

Maharshi Dhondo Keshav Karve, also known as "Maharshi Karve," was a pioneering social reformer and educator in 20th-century India, renowned for his tireless efforts in promoting women's education and empowerment. His visionary initiatives transformed the landscape of women's education in India and laid the foundation for gender equality and social progress.

Early Life and Background

Maharshi Dhondo Keshav Karve, a luminary in the realm of social reform, was born on April 18, 1858, in the quaint village of Sheravali, nestled in the heart of Maharashtra, India. His arrival into this world marked the inception of a journey that would significantly alter the socio-cultural landscape of India, particularly in the realm of women's empowerment and education.

Hailing from a lineage steeped in the traditions of Brahminism, Karve's early years were enveloped in the sanctity of traditional Brahmin values and customs. Raised amidst the resplendent echoes of Vedic hymns and the solemn recitations of ancient scriptures, he imbibed the essence of Sanskrit wisdom from an early age. The sacred verses of the Vedas and the timeless teachings of Hindu scriptures served as the foundational pillars upon which his intellectual edifice was erected.

Yet, beneath the veneer of traditionalism lay a fervent spirit of inquiry and a relentless pursuit of knowledge. Karve's inquisitive mind sought to traverse beyond the confines of orthodoxy, venturing into the realms of rationality and social consciousness. It was this innate curiosity coupled with an unwavering commitment to social reform that laid the groundwork for his transformative endeavors in the years to come.

As he embarked on his educational journey, Karve's scholarly pursuits mirrored the dichotomy of his upbringing. While he delved deep into the intricacies of Sanskrit grammar and the nuances of Hindu philosophy, his academic pursuits were imbued with a profound sense of social responsibility. He recognized education not merely as a means of intellectual enlightenment but as a potent instrument for societal change.

The confluence of traditional learning and progressive ideals paved the way for Karve's burgeoning activism in the realm of women's rights. Witnessing firsthand the pervasive inequities and systemic injustices faced by women in Indian society, he was propelled into action, determined to challenge the entrenched patriarchal norms that stifled their potential.

Karve's advocacy for women's rights found fertile ground amidst the burgeoning social reform movements of late 19th-century India. Inspired by the pioneering efforts of social reformers like Raja Ram Mohan Roy and Jyotirao Phule, he embarked on a crusade to dismantle the age-old shackles of oppression and usher in an era of gender equality and empowerment.

Central to Karve's vision of social reform was the pivotal role of education in emancipating women from the chains of ignorance and subjugation. He fervently believed that education was the cornerstone upon which the edifice of gender equality could be erected, empowering women to chart their own destinies and participate as equals in the socio-political sphere.

Driven by this conviction, Karve spearheaded numerous initiatives aimed at expanding educational opportunities for women across India. His pioneering efforts culminated in the establishment of the first women's school in Pune in 1896, heralding a new dawn in the realm of female education. This seminal institution served as a beacon of hope for countless women, offering them the tools to transcend the constraints of their circumstances and carve out a place for themselves in society.

Karve's tireless advocacy for women's education was not confined to the realms of academia; it permeated every facet of his life. As a devoted husband and father, he espoused progressive ideals within the confines of his own household, ensuring that his daughters received the same level of education and opportunity as his sons. In doing so, he exemplified the principles of gender equality and set a precedent for future generations to emulate.

Despite facing vehement opposition from conservative quarters, Karve remained steadfast in his commitment to the cause of women's empowerment. His unwavering resolve and indomitable spirit served as a source of inspiration for countless individuals, igniting a spark of hope in the hearts of those yearning for change.

Karve's legacy continues to reverberate through the corridors of time, transcending the confines of temporal boundaries. His pioneering efforts in the realm of women's education laid the groundwork for subsequent generations of social reformers, paving the way for the gradual dismantling of patriarchal structures and the empowerment of women across India.

In commemorating the life and legacy of Maharshi Dhondo Keshav Karve, we pay homage to a visionary whose indelible imprint on the annals of history serves as a testament to the enduring power of human perseverance and the transformative potential of social reform. As we reflect on his remarkable journey, let us draw inspiration from his unwavering commitment to justice and equality, and strive to carry forth the mantle of his noble crusade into the future.

Advocacy for Women's Rights

Maharshi Dhondo Keshav Karve emerged as a beacon of enlightenment in an era fraught with deep-rooted prejudices and entrenched patriarchal norms. Born into a society where women were relegated to the margins of existence, denied even the most fundamental rights and opportunities, Karve was acutely aware of the systemic injustices that pervaded every facet of their lives. It was against this backdrop of pervasive inequality and oppression that he embarked on a fervent crusade to dismantle the barriers that stifled the potential of half the population.

Karve's advocacy for women's rights was not merely a product of intellectual contemplation but a visceral response to the glaring inequities he witnessed in his daily life. From the confines of his own household to the broader canvas of Indian society, he bore witness to the myriad ways in which women were systematically disenfranchised and marginalized. Denied access to education, barred from participating in decision-making processes, and relegated to subordinate roles within the domestic sphere, women bore the brunt of centuries-old customs and traditions that perpetuated their subjugation.

Central to Karve's advocacy was the recognition that the emancipation of women was not merely a moral imperative but a pragmatic necessity for societal progress and development. He understood that the exclusion of women from the realms of education and employment not only deprived them of their inherent rights but also stunted the socio-economic growth of the nation as a whole. By relegating women to the confines of domesticity, society squandered the immense reservoir of talent and potential they possessed, hindering the realization of a more equitable and prosperous future.

Karve's advocacy for women's rights was multifaceted, encompassing a wide array of initiatives aimed at challenging the status quo and effecting tangible change. At the forefront of his efforts was the promotion of women's education as a catalyst for empowerment and emancipation. Recognizing education as the cornerstone upon which the edifice of gender equality could be erected, he tirelessly campaigned for the establishment of schools and colleges for girls, ensuring that they had access to the same educational opportunities as their male counterparts.

The establishment of the first women's school in Pune in 1896 marked a watershed moment in the history of women's education in

India, heralding a new era of possibility and promise. This seminal institution, founded under the auspices of Karve's visionary leadership, served as a beacon of hope for countless women across the nation, offering them the tools to break free from the shackles of ignorance and assert their rightful place in society. Through education, Karve sought to instill in women a sense of self-worth and agency, empowering them to challenge the prevailing orthodoxy and carve out their own destinies.

Yet, Karve's advocacy extended far beyond the realm of education, encompassing a broader spectrum of issues that affected women's lives. He vehemently opposed practices such as child marriage and widowhood, which robbed women of their autonomy and agency, condemning them to a lifetime of servitude and suffering. Through his writings and speeches, he sought to raise awareness about the inherent injustice of such practices, galvanizing public opinion and mobilizing support for their abolition.

Karve's advocacy for women's rights was characterized by a nuanced understanding of the intersecting oppressions that women faced based on their caste, class, and socio-economic status. He recognized that women belonging to marginalized communities were doubly marginalized, facing compounded forms of discrimination and exploitation. In response, he sought to address the root causes of their oppression, advocating for comprehensive social reforms that would uplift the most vulnerable segments of society.

One of the most enduring legacies of Karve's advocacy for women's rights was his pioneering efforts in the realm of widow remarriage. In a society where widowhood was equated with social death, consigning women to a life of perpetual mourning and ostracism, he sought to challenge the prevailing taboos and stigma surrounding widow remarriage. Through his relentless advocacy and tireless lobbying, he succeeded in overturning centuries-old customs and securing legal reforms that granted widows the right to remarry, thereby restoring their dignity and autonomy.

Karve's advocacy for women's rights was not without its challenges and setbacks. He faced vehement opposition from conservative quarters, who viewed his progressive ideals as a threat to the established order. Yet, undeterred by the forces of reaction and resistance, he pressed forward with unwavering determination, fueled by a steadfast belief in the inherent righteousness of his cause.

In commemorating the life and legacy of Maharshi Dhondo Keshav Karve, we pay homage to a visionary whose tireless advocacy paved the way for the empowerment of women across India. His indomitable spirit and unwavering commitment to justice continue to inspire generations of social reformers, reminding us of the transformative power of human agency in the ongoing struggle for equality and justice. As we reflect on his remarkable journey, let us draw inspiration from his example and rededicate ourselves to the noble cause of women's rights, ensuring that his legacy endures as a beacon of hope for generations to come.

Founding of Hingane Stree Shikshan Samstha:

In the annals of India's rich tapestry of social reform movements, few endeavors stand as testament to the transformative power of education and empowerment as the founding of the Hingane Stree Shikshan Samstha by Maharshi Dhondo Keshav Karve. Established in the bustling city of Pune, Maharashtra, in the year 1896, the Samstha emerged as a beacon of hope for widows and destitute women, offering them not only the gift of education but also the promise of a brighter future filled with dignity and self-reliance.

At the heart of Maharshi Karve's vision for the Hingane Stree Shikshan Samstha lay a profound commitment to social justice and gender equality. He recognized that women, particularly widows and those marginalized by society, faced systemic barriers that prevented them from accessing education and economic opportunities. Denied the right to remarry and ostracized by their communities, these women languished on the fringes of society, bereft of agency and autonomy.

The establishment of the Samstha represented a radical departure from the prevailing norms and practices that relegated women to the confines of domesticity and servitude. It was a bold assertion of their inherent worth and potential, a declaration that every woman, regardless of her circumstances, deserved the opportunity to thrive and prosper. Through education and vocational training, Maharshi Karve sought to empower these marginalized women, equipping them with the skills and knowledge necessary to chart their own destinies and break free from the cycle of poverty and dependence.

The founding principles of the Hingane Stree Shikshan Samstha were rooted in the ethos of empowerment and self-reliance. Recognizing that education alone was not sufficient to uplift marginalized women, Maharshi Karve envisioned a holistic approach that combined academic instruction with vocational training, enabling women to acquire both intellectual and practical skills. By imparting training in fields such as sewing, weaving, and nursing, the Samstha sought to equip women with the means to earn a livelihood and support themselves and their families.

Central to the Samstha's mission was the promotion of women's autonomy and agency. Unlike traditional charitable institutions that perpetuated a paternalistic approach to social welfare, the Samstha operated on the principles of self-help and collective empowerment. Women were not merely passive recipients of aid but active participants in their own liberation, taking ownership of their education and livelihoods and working together to forge a path towards economic independence.

The impact of the Hingane Stree Shikshan Samstha extended far beyond the confines of its walls, rippling outward to transform the lives of countless women and communities across Maharashtra. Through its innovative programs and initiatives, the Samstha became a catalyst for social change, challenging entrenched notions of gender roles and reshaping the contours of public discourse on women's rights and empowerment.

One of the most enduring legacies of the Samstha was its emphasis on community engagement and grassroots activism. Recognizing that sustainable change could only be achieved through collective action, Maharshi Karve fostered strong ties with local communities and forged partnerships with like-minded individuals and organizations. Together, they mobilized support for women's education and empowerment, rallying behind the Samstha's mission with unwavering dedication and resolve.

The success of the Hingane Stree Shikshan Samstha served as a powerful testament to the transformative potential of grassroots initiatives in effecting social change. By empowering marginalized women to become agents of change within their own communities, the Samstha laid the groundwork for a more equitable and just society, where every individual, regardless of gender or social status, had the opportunity to realize their full potential.

Maharshi Karve's founding of the Hingane Stree Shikshan Samstha was more than a mere philanthropic endeavor; it was a revolutionary act of resistance against the prevailing norms of his time. In challenging the entrenched patriarchy and caste hierarchy that perpetuated the subjugation of women, he struck at the very heart of the social order, heralding a new era of possibility and promise for generations of women to come.

As we reflect on the founding of the Hingane Stree Shikshan Samstha and the legacy of Maharshi Dhondo Keshav Karve, we are reminded of the enduring power of education and empowerment to transform lives and uplift communities. His visionary leadership and unwavering commitment to social justice continue to inspire us to strive for a more inclusive and equitable society, where every individual, regardless of gender or background, has the opportunity to flourish and thrive.

Development of Widow Education

Maharshi Dhondo Keshav Karve's visionary approach to social reform encompassed a deep-seated commitment to addressing the plight of widows in Indian society. In an era marked by pervasive social stigma, economic deprivation, and limited opportunities for education and employment, widows occupied a particularly vulnerable position, consigned to a life of perpetual mourning and marginalization. Yet, it was against this backdrop of entrenched prejudice and systemic injustice that Karve envisioned a future where widows could reclaim their agency and lead lives of dignity and self-reliance.

Central to Karve's vision for the empowerment of widows was the recognition that education held the key to unlocking their potential and enabling them to chart their own destinies. He understood that the denial of education was not only a symptom of their marginalization but also a perpetuator of their dependence and vulnerability. By equipping widows with the tools of knowledge and skill, Karve sought to break the cycle of poverty and oppression that ensnared them, empowering them to transcend the limitations imposed upon them by society.

To address the multifaceted challenges faced by widows, Karve embarked on a pioneering initiative that would come to be known as the Widows' Home in Hingane, Pune. Founded on the principles of compassion, dignity, and self-reliance, the Widows' Home served as a sanctuary for widows seeking refuge from the harsh realities of their circumstances. More than merely a shelter, it was a transformative space where widows were afforded the opportunity to rebuild their lives and reclaim their sense of agency.

At the heart of the Widows' Home was its emphasis on education as a means of empowerment and liberation. Recognizing that education was the cornerstone upon which the edifice of gender equality could be erected, Karve ensured that widows residing in the Home had access to formal schooling and vocational training. Through a comprehensive curriculum that encompassed both academic instruction and practical skills development, widows were equipped with the tools necessary to secure gainful employment and achieve economic independence.

The educational programs offered at the Widows' Home were tailored to the unique needs and aspirations of its residents, recognizing that each widow brought with her a wealth of untapped potential and talent. From literacy classes and sewing workshops to courses in nursing and bookkeeping, the curriculum was designed to provide widows with a diverse array of skills and competencies that would enhance their employability and broaden their horizons.

Yet, the Widows' Home was more than just a place of learning; it was a vibrant community where widows found solace, solidarity, and support. Through collective activities such as gardening, handicrafts, and cultural events, residents forged bonds of friendship and camaraderie, creating a sense of belonging that transcended the confines of their individual circumstances. In this nurturing environment, widows were able to overcome the isolation and loneliness that often accompanied widowhood, finding strength and resilience in the company of their peers.

The impact of the Widows' Home extended far beyond its physical walls, rippling outward to transform the lives of widows and communities across Maharashtra. Through its innovative programs and initiatives, it became a model of best practices in the field of widow education and empowerment, inspiring similar initiatives to spring up in other parts of the country. By demonstrating the transformative power of education and empowerment, the Widows' Home challenged entrenched notions of gender roles and reshaped the contours of public discourse on women's rights and dignity.

One of the most enduring legacies of the Widows' Home was its role in challenging the prevailing stigma surrounding widowhood and advocating for the rights and dignity of widows. In a society where widowhood was often equated with social death, consigning women to a life of perpetual mourning and ostracism, the Home provided a counter-narrative of resilience and empowerment. Through its emphasis on education and self-reliance, it sought to dismantle the age-old customs and traditions that perpetuated the marginalization of widows, paving the way for a more inclusive and compassionate society.

Maharshi Karve's development of widow education through the establishment of the Widows' Home stands as a testament to his unwavering commitment to social justice and gender equality. In providing widows with the tools of knowledge and skill, he not only empowered them to improve their own lives but also catalyzed a broader movement for social change. Through his visionary leadership and tireless advocacy, he laid the groundwork for a more just and equitable society, where every individual, regardless of gender or social status, has the opportunity to flourish and thrive.

As we reflect on the legacy of Maharshi Dhondo Keshav Karve and the development of widow education, we are reminded of the enduring power of education to transform lives and uplift communities. His pioneering efforts in this field serve as a beacon of hope for generations to come, inspiring us to strive for a world where every individual is afforded the opportunity to realize their full potential and live a life of dignity and fulfillment.

Expansion of Educational Initiatives

Maharshi Dhondo Keshav Karve's relentless pursuit of women's empowerment and education found its fullest expression in the expansion of educational initiatives under the auspices of the Hingane Stree Shikshan Samstha. From its humble beginnings as a beacon of hope for widows and destitute women, the Samstha evolved into a comprehensive educational institution, offering a wide range of programs catering to the diverse needs and aspirations of women and girls from all walks of life. Under Karve's visionary leadership, the Samstha embarked on a transformative journey that would forever alter the educational landscape of Maharashtra.

At the core of the Samstha's educational philosophy was the belief that education was the key to unlocking the full potential of women and enabling them to lead lives of dignity and self-reliance. Karve understood that access to quality education was not merely a privilege but a fundamental human right, essential for the realization of individual aspirations and the collective progress of society. Guided by this ethos, the Samstha sought to democratize education and make it accessible to women from all strata of society, regardless of their socio-economic background.

One of the most significant achievements of the Samstha was the establishment of a network of schools and colleges that provided women with opportunities for formal education and academic advancement. These institutions, scattered across rural and urban areas alike, served as oases of learning and enlightenment, offering a curriculum that combined academic excellence with a strong emphasis on practical skills development. From basic literacy classes to advanced courses in subjects such as literature, science, and commerce, the Samstha's educational offerings catered to the diverse interests and aptitudes of its students.

In addition to traditional academic subjects, the Samstha also placed a strong emphasis on vocational training, recognizing the importance of equipping women with the skills necessary to thrive in a rapidly changing economic landscape. To this end, it established vocational training centers that offered courses in fields such as sewing, embroidery, agriculture, and animal husbandry. These programs not only provided women with valuable skills for employment but also fostered a sense of self-confidence and empowerment, enabling them to become active participants in their communities.

The expansion of educational initiatives under the Hingane Stree Shikshan Samstha was guided by a commitment to inclusivity and diversity, ensuring that women from marginalized communities were not left behind. Recognizing the intersecting oppressions faced by women based on their caste, class, and socio-economic status, the Samstha implemented targeted outreach programs to reach those most in need. Mobile education vans traversed remote villages and tribal areas, bringing education to the doorsteps of women who had long been excluded from the benefits of formal schooling.

One of the hallmarks of the Samstha's educational initiatives was its focus on holistic development, encompassing not only intellectual growth but also physical, emotional, and social well-being. Through extracurricular activities such as sports, arts, and cultural events, students were encouraged to explore their talents and interests, fostering a sense of camaraderie and camaraderie that transcended the boundaries of the classroom. Additionally, the Samstha provided counseling and support services to address the unique challenges faced by women, including issues related to health, family, and personal development.

The impact of the Samstha's educational initiatives was profound and far-reaching, transforming the lives of countless women and communities across Maharashtra. By providing women with access to quality education and vocational training, it empowered them to break free from the cycle of poverty and dependence, enabling them to become agents of change within their families and communities. Graduates of the Samstha's programs went on to pursue careers in fields such as education, healthcare, agriculture, and entrepreneurship, contributing to the socio-economic development of the region.

One of the most enduring legacies of the Samstha's educational initiatives was its role in challenging entrenched gender norms and stereotypes that limited the aspirations and opportunities of women. Through its emphasis on women's education and empowerment, it sought to redefine notions of femininity and masculinity, promoting a more egalitarian and inclusive vision of society. By demonstrating the inherent capabilities and potential of women, the Samstha inspired a new generation of leaders and change-makers who would continue to push the boundaries of what was possible for women in Indian society.

As we reflect on the expansion of educational initiatives under the

Hingane Stree Shikshan Samstha and the legacy of Maharshi Dhondo Keshav Karve, we are reminded of the transformative power of education to uplift individuals and communities. His visionary leadership and unwavering commitment to social justice continue to inspire us to strive for a world where every individual, regardless of gender or background, has the opportunity to realize their full potential and lead a life of dignity and fulfillment.

Founding of Shreemati Nathibai Damodar Thackersey Women's University

In the annals of India's educational history, the founding of the Shreemati Nathibai Damodar Thackersey Women's University (SNDT Women's University) in Mumbai, Maharashtra, stands as a watershed moment, marking a paradigm shift in the landscape of women's education and empowerment. Conceived in 1916 by the visionary social reformer Maharshi Dhondo Keshav Karve, the university emerged as a beacon of hope and opportunity for generations of women, offering them the chance to pursue higher education and professional training in a supportive and inclusive environment.

At the heart of Maharshi Karve's vision for SNDT Women's University lay a deep-seated commitment to advancing the cause of women's education and empowerment. He recognized that access to higher education was not merely a privilege but a fundamental human right, essential for the realization of individual aspirations and the collective progress of society. Guided by this ethos, he embarked on a bold endeavor to establish a university exclusively for women, where they could pursue their academic and professional ambitions free from the constraints of gender discrimination and social prejudice.

The founding of SNDT Women's University represented a bold departure from the prevailing norms of the time, which relegated women to subordinate roles within the domestic sphere and denied them access to higher education. By establishing the first women's university in India, Maharshi Karve sought to challenge entrenched notions of gender inequality and create a space where women could thrive intellectually, socially, and professionally. The university was named in honor of Shreemati Nathibai Damodar Thackersey, a pioneering advocate for women's education in India, whose legacy inspired generations of women to pursue their dreams.

From its humble beginnings as a small institution offering courses in teacher training and social work, SNDT Women's University quickly expanded its offerings to include a wide range of academic disciplines and professional programs. Under Maharshi Karve's visionary leadership, the university became a hub of intellectual and cultural exchange, attracting students from across India and beyond who were drawn to its progressive ethos and commitment to excellence.

One of the defining features of SNDT Women's University was its emphasis on providing women with opportunities for holistic development, encompassing not only academic excellence but also personal growth and leadership development. Through a diverse array of extracurricular activities, including sports, arts, and community service, students were encouraged to explore their talents and interests, fostering a sense of confidence and self-esteem that would serve them well in their future endeavors.

SNDT Women's University played a pivotal role in advancing women's education and leadership in India, producing a generation of trailblazing women who went on to make significant contributions to society in various fields. Graduates of the university have excelled as educators, social workers, healthcare professionals, scientists, entrepreneurs, and leaders in government and civil society, leaving an indelible mark on the fabric of Indian society.

In addition to its academic programs, SNDT Women's University also played a pioneering role in promoting research and scholarship on issues related to women's empowerment and gender equality. Through its research centers and institutes, faculty and students engaged in groundbreaking research that shed light on the unique challenges faced by women in India and explored innovative solutions to address them. The university's commitment to research and scholarship continues to drive forward the agenda for gender equality and social justice in India.

Over the years, SNDT Women's University has evolved into a dynamic and vibrant institution, adapting to the changing needs and aspirations of women in the 21st century. It has embraced new technologies and pedagogical approaches to enhance the learning experience for its students, while also remaining true to its founding principles of inclusivity, diversity, and social responsibility. Today, SNDT Women's University stands as a shining example of what is possible when women are given the opportunity to pursue their dreams and fulfill their potential.

As we reflect on the founding of SNDT Women's University and the legacy of Maharshi Dhondo Keshav Karve, we are reminded of the transformative power of education to uplift individuals and communities. His visionary leadership and unwavering commitment to social justice continue to inspire us to strive for a world where every woman has the opportunity to realize her full potential and contribute to the advancement of society. SNDT Women's University remains a beacon of empowerment for women across India, embodying the spirit of resilience, determination, and hope that defines the journey towards gender equality.

Advocacy for Social Reform

Maharshi Dhondo Keshav Karve stands as an indomitable figure in the annals of Indian history, revered not only for his pioneering contributions to women's education but also for his unwavering commitment to social reform. Throughout his illustrious career as a social reformer and educator, Karve tirelessly campaigned against entrenched injustices and discriminatory practices that plagued Indian society, advocating for gender equality, social justice, and human rights.

At the heart of Karve's advocacy for social reform was his steadfast belief in the inherent dignity and equality of all individuals. Born into a society rife with caste prejudices, gender biases, and socio-economic disparities, he bore witness to the pervasive inequalities and injustices that afflicted the lives of millions of Indians. Determined to challenge the status quo and usher in a more just and equitable society, Karve embarked on a lifelong crusade to dismantle the barriers that perpetuated social inequality and oppression.

One of the most pressing issues that Karve confronted in his advocacy for social reform was the scourge of child marriage. In a society where the practice of child marriage was widespread, consigning young girls to lives of premature motherhood and servitude, he recognized the urgent need to challenge the prevailing norms and customs that sanctioned such practices. Through his writings, speeches, and grassroots activism, Karve sought to raise awareness about the detrimental effects of child marriage on the health, education, and well-being of girls, galvanizing public opinion and mobilizing support for legal reforms to abolish this archaic practice.

Similarly, Karve vehemently opposed the practice of dowry, which perpetuated gender inequality and economic exploitation within families. He recognized that dowry not only commodified women's bodies but also reinforced patriarchal norms that relegated them to subordinate roles within the household. Through his advocacy, Karve sought to challenge the entrenched customs and traditions that upheld the institution of dowry, advocating for legal reforms and social sanctions to eradicate this pernicious practice once and for all.

Caste discrimination was another issue that occupied a central place in Karve's advocacy for social reform. As a staunch opponent of the caste system, he viewed caste-based discrimination as antithetical to the principles of equality and justice enshrined in the Indian Constitution. Through his writings and speeches, Karve denounced the insidious effects of caste prejudice and untouchability, calling for a concerted effort to eradicate these deeply entrenched social evils from the fabric of Indian society. He believed that true progress could only be achieved by fostering a spirit of unity and solidarity among all sections of society, transcending the artificial barriers of caste and creed that divided them.

Karve's advocacy for social reform was not limited to theoretical discourse or intellectual debate; it was grounded in practical action and grassroots mobilization. He recognized that meaningful change could only be achieved through collective action and community empowerment. To this end, he established a network of social reform organizations and grassroots movements aimed at mobilizing public opinion and effecting tangible change at the grassroots level. Through initiatives such as the Widows' Home, the Hingane Stree Shikshan Samstha, and the Shreemati Nathibai Damodar Thackersey Women's University, Karve sought to create spaces where individuals could come together to challenge the prevailing norms and practices that perpetuated social inequality and injustice.

Karve's advocacy for social reform was characterized by a holistic approach that addressed the root causes of social injustice and oppression. He understood that true progress could only be achieved by addressing the interconnected issues of poverty, discrimination, and lack of access to education and opportunities. Through his multifaceted approach to social reform, Karve sought to create a more just and equitable society where every individual, regardless of gender, caste, or social status, could realize their full potential and lead lives of dignity and fulfillment.

The legacy of Maharshi Dhondo Keshav Karve's advocacy for social reform continues to reverberate through the corridors of time, inspiring future generations to carry forth the mantle of his noble crusade. In commemorating his remarkable contributions to the cause of social justice and human rights, we honor not only the man but the enduring ideals of equality, justice, and compassion that he espoused. As we strive to build a more inclusive and equitable society, let us draw inspiration from his example and rededicate ourselves to the noble task of creating a world where every individual is afforded the opportunity to flourish and thrive.

Recognition and Legacy

The legacy of Maharshi Dhondo Keshav Karve transcends the confines of time and space, enduring as a beacon of hope and inspiration for generations to come. His tireless dedication to the cause of women's education and social reform earned him widespread recognition and acclaim, both in his native land of India and across the globe. From the humble confines of his classroom to the hallowed halls of academia and beyond, Maharshi Karve's transformative vision continues to shape the contours of our collective consciousness, reminding us of the transformative power of human compassion and the enduring legacy of social change.

Born into a society fraught with entrenched prejudices and systemic inequalities, Maharshi Karve's journey towards enlightenment was marked by a steadfast commitment to justice, equality, and human dignity. From an early age, he witnessed firsthand the injustices and inequities that plagued Indian society, particularly with regard to the status of women. Determined to challenge the prevailing norms and customs that perpetuated their subjugation, Karve embarked on a lifelong quest to empower women through education and social reform.

It was Maharshi Karve's unwavering dedication to the cause of women's education that earned him the enduring title of "Maharshi" (Great Sage) by the people of Maharashtra. This esteemed honor, bestowed upon him in recognition of his exemplary service to society, encapsulates the profound impact of his work and the reverence with which he was held by his peers and contemporaries. Through his pioneering efforts to establish educational institutions and advocate for social change, Maharshi Karve emerged as a towering figure in the annals of Indian history, leaving an indelible mark on the collective consciousness of the nation.

In 1958, Maharshi Dhondo Keshav Karve's unparalleled contributions to women's education and social reform were further affirmed when he was honored with the Bharat Ratna, India's highest civilian award. This prestigious accolade, bestowed upon him by the Government of India, served as a testament to his lifelong dedication to the cause of women's empowerment and social justice. As one of the earliest recipients of this esteemed honor, Maharshi Karve's legacy was cemented in the annals of Indian history, ensuring that his contributions would be remembered and celebrated for generations to come.

Maharshi Karve's legacy extends far beyond the accolades and honors bestowed upon him during his lifetime. It lives on in the countless lives he touched and the communities he transformed through his visionary leadership and unwavering commitment to social reform. From the establishment of the first women's school in Pune to the founding of the Shreemati Nathibai Damodar Thackersey Women's University in Mumbai, Maharshi Karve's legacy is etched into the very fabric of Indian society, shaping the lives and aspirations of millions of women across the nation.

One of the most enduring aspects of Maharshi Karve's legacy is his profound impact on the field of women's education in India. Through his pioneering efforts to establish educational institutions and advocate for equal access to education, he laid the foundation for the empowerment of generations of women. Today, the institutions founded by Maharshi Karve continue to thrive as centers of academic excellence and innovation, providing women with the knowledge, skills, and opportunities they need to succeed in a rapidly changing world.

Beyond his contributions to women's education, Maharshi Karve's legacy is also evident in his advocacy for social reform and human rights. Throughout his life, he campaigned tirelessly against practices such as child marriage, dowry, and caste discrimination, which perpetuated social inequality and oppression. Through his writings, speeches, and grassroots activism, he sought to raise awareness about the detrimental effects of these practices and mobilize support for legal reforms to abolish them.

Maharshi Karve's legacy continues to inspire generations of social reformers and educators who strive to create a more just, equitable, and inclusive society for all. His unwavering dedication to the cause of women's education and social reform serves as a shining example of the transformative power of compassion, courage, and perseverance. As we reflect on his remarkable life and contributions, we are reminded of the enduring impact that one individual can have on the world, and the profound responsibility we all share to work towards a better future for generations to come.

Conclusion

In conclusion, Maharshi Dhondo Keshav Karve's contributions to women's education and social reform were instrumental in challenging oppressive customs and empowering women in 20th-century India. His pioneering initiatives, including the establishment of the Hingane Stree Shikshan Samstha and SNDT Women's University, transformed the educational landscape for women and laid the foundation for their empowerment and participation in society. Maharshi Kar

3. 3 - Tarabai Shinde

Tarabai Shinde was a pioneering figure in the fight for women's rights in India during the late 19th and early 20th centuries. Her writings and activism challenged prevailing social norms and patriarchal structures, advocating for women's education, autonomy, and equality. In this essay, we delve into the life and legacy of Tarabai Shinde, exploring her contributions to the women's movement in India and her enduring impact on feminist thought.

Early Life and Background:

Tarabai Shinde's life unfolded against the backdrop of 19th-century Maharashtra, a time when rigid caste hierarchies and patriarchal norms defined the social fabric of Indian society. Born in 1850 into a Brahmin family in Maharashtra, India, Shinde's early years were shrouded in obscurity, with little information available about her formative experiences and upbringing. Nevertheless, her trajectory as a pioneering social reformer and advocate for women's rights bears testament to the profound impact of her socio-cultural milieu on shaping her worldview and values.

Growing up in a society marked by entrenched inequalities and pervasive discrimination, Shinde would have been acutely aware of the myriad challenges faced by women in her time. From a young age, she would have been confronted with the stark reality of gender-based oppression and the limited opportunities available to women for education and self-expression. However, far from being resigned to the status quo, Shinde exhibited a keen intellect and a fiery spirit of defiance, laying the foundation for her future activism and advocacy.

While specific details about Shinde's early life remain elusive, it is evident that she emerged as a trailblazer in the field of social reform, challenging prevailing norms and conventions through her writings and activism. In a society where women's voices were often silenced and their experiences marginalized, Shinde dared to speak out against the injustices perpetrated against her gender, laying bare the hypocrisy and double standards that underpinned patriarchal society.

At a time when women were relegated to the margins of public life and denied access to formal education, Shinde's advocacy for women's rights was both radical and revolutionary. Drawing inspiration from her own lived experiences and observations of the world around her, she articulated a powerful critique of the oppressive structures that constrained women's lives, calling for nothing less than a wholesale transformation of society's attitudes towards gender and caste.

Central to Shinde's advocacy was her insistence on the inherent dignity and agency of women, challenging prevailing notions of female inferiority and subservience. Through her writings, she sought to debunk the myths and stereotypes that justified women's subjugation, highlighting the intellectual and moral capabilities of her gender and demanding their rightful place in society as equals.

Shinde's early experiences in a society characterized by rigid caste hierarchies would have also shaped her understanding of intersectional oppression and the interconnected nature of social injustice. As a Brahmin woman, she would have been acutely aware of the privileges afforded to her by virtue of her caste status, even as she sought to challenge the patriarchal norms that constrained her gender. This awareness of the complex dynamics of power and privilege would inform her later activism and advocacy, as she sought to forge solidarity across caste and gender lines in pursuit of a more just and equitable society.

While the specifics of Shinde's early life remain shrouded in mystery, her emergence as a leading voice in the struggle for women's rights speaks to the transformative power of individual agency and resistance. Against the backdrop of a society rife with injustice and inequality, she dared to imagine a world where women could live free from the shackles of oppression, their voices heard and their aspirations realized. In this sense, Shinde's early life and background serve as a powerful reminder of the indomitable spirit of those who dare to challenge the status quo and envision a more just and equitable future for all.

Writings and Activism:

Tarabai Shinde's legacy as a pioneering feminist thinker and social reformer is anchored in her seminal work, "Stri Purush Tulana" (A Comparison Between Women and Men), published in 1882. This groundbreaking essay represents a watershed moment in the history of Indian feminism, challenging entrenched patriarchal norms and advocating for gender equality and women's emancipation. Through her incisive analysis and impassioned advocacy, Shinde emerged as a fearless champion of women's rights, laying the groundwork for a more just and equitable society.

In "Stri Purush Tulana, " Shinde offers a scathing critique of the unequal treatment of women in Indian society, exposing the myriad injustices and indignities they endure on account of their gender. Drawing on a diverse range of sources, including personal experiences, historical examples, and philosophical insights, she meticulously deconstructs prevailing myths and stereotypes about women's inferiority, arguing for their equal rights and dignity.

One of the central themes of Shinde's essay is the pervasive discrimination faced by women in various spheres of life, including education, marriage, and social status. She highlights the systemic barriers that prevent women from accessing education and pursuing their intellectual and professional aspirations, condemning the prevailing norms and attitudes that relegate them to subordinate roles within the household and society at large.

Shinde's critique of gender inequality extends beyond the realm of education to encompass broader social and cultural practices that perpetuate women's subjugation. She denounces the institution of marriage as a site of exploitation and oppression, where women are treated as mere objects of exchange and subjected to the dictates of patriarchal authority. Through vivid anecdotes and compelling arguments, Shinde exposes the hypocrisies and injustices inherent in the institution of marriage, calling for its transformation into a partnership based on mutual respect and equality.

Central to Shinde's argument is her insistence on the inherent dignity and agency of women, challenging prevailing notions of female inferiority and subservience. She rejects the notion that women are inherently weak or irrational, asserting their intellectual and moral capabilities on par with men. By affirming women's inherent worth and potential, Shinde lays the foundation for a more egalitarian and inclusive vision of society, where gender does not determine one's worth or opportunities.

In addition to her critique of gender inequality, Shinde also offers a profound analysis of the intersecting oppressions faced by women based on factors such as caste and class. She recognizes that women from marginalized communities are doubly oppressed, facing discrimination not only on the basis of their gender but also their caste or socio-economic status. Through her writings and activism,

Shinde seeks to amplify the voices of these marginalized women and challenge the intersecting systems of oppression that constrain their lives.

Shinde's writings were not merely intellectual exercises but were deeply intertwined with her activism and advocacy for social change. She understood the power of words to challenge prevailing norms and inspire collective action, using her platform as a writer to galvanize support for women's rights and emancipation. Through public lectures, pamphlets, and grassroots organizing, Shinde sought to mobilize women from all walks of life to demand their rightful place in society and assert their agency and autonomy.

Despite facing backlash and criticism from conservative quarters, Shinde remained steadfast in her commitment to women's empowerment and social justice. She was unafraid to confront entrenched power structures and challenge the status quo, even at great personal risk. Her courage and resilience in the face of adversity serve as a testament to her unwavering dedication to the cause of gender equality and women's emancipation.

Shinde's activism extended beyond the realm of gender to encompass broader social issues, including caste discrimination and social reform. She understood that true liberation could only be achieved by addressing the intersecting oppressions faced by women based on factors such as caste, class, and religion. Through her writings and activism, she sought to build solidarity across diverse communities and forge alliances in the struggle against all forms of oppression and injustice.

In her later years, Shinde continued to be a vocal advocate for social reform, tirelessly championing the cause of women's rights until her death in 1910. While her life was tragically cut short, her legacy endures as a beacon of hope and inspiration for future generations of feminists and social reformers. Through her writings and activism, Shinde paved the way for a more just and equitable society, where all individuals are afforded the opportunity to realize their full potential, regardless of gender, caste, or social status.

Critique of Patriarchy and Social Norms

Tarabai Shinde's seminal work, "Stri Purush Tulana, " stands as a powerful indictment of patriarchy and the oppressive social norms that perpetuate gender inequality in Indian society. Published in 1882, this groundbreaking essay represents a courageous and incisive critique of the entrenched systems of power and privilege that privilege men at the expense of women. Through her penetrating analysis and uncompromising advocacy, Shinde exposes the double standards and hypocrisy that underpin the treatment of women, challenging the prevailing norms and conventions that relegate them to subordinate roles within the household and society at large.

At the heart of Shinde's critique is her interrogation of the institution of patriarchy, which she identifies as the root cause of women's oppression. Patriarchy, as Shinde defines it, is a system of social organization characterized by male dominance and female subordination, where power and authority are concentrated in the hands of men, to the detriment of women's rights and autonomy. Through her writings, she lays bare the ways in which patriarchy operates to uphold the status quo, perpetuating gender inequality and stifling women's agency and self-expression.

One of the central themes of "Stri Purush Tulana" is Shinde's critique of the unequal treatment of women in various spheres of life, including marriage, education, and religious practices. She exposes the myriad injustices and indignities faced by women within the institution of marriage, where they are often treated as mere objects of exchange and subjected to the dictates of patriarchal authority. Shinde argues that women's subordinate status within marriage reflects broader societal attitudes towards gender, which privilege men's interests and desires over those of women.

In her critique of marriage, Shinde highlights the ways in which women are denied agency and autonomy, forced to conform to societal expectations and fulfill prescribed gender roles. She challenges the notion of marriage as a partnership based on mutual respect and equality, instead portraying it as a site of exploitation and oppression, where women are expected to sacrifice their own desires and aspirations for the sake of familial harmony and social conformity. Through vivid anecdotes and compelling arguments, Shinde calls for a radical reimagining of marriage as a relationship grounded in equality and mutual consent, where women are afforded the same rights and freedoms as men.

Education emerges as another key site of contention in Shinde's critique of patriarchy and social norms. She highlights the systemic barriers that prevent women from accessing education and pursuing their intellectual and professional aspirations, condemning the prevailing norms and attitudes that relegate them to subordinate roles within the household and society at large. Shinde argues that education is not only a fundamental human right but also a means of empowerment and liberation for women, enabling them to challenge existing power structures and assert their rights and autonomy.

Through her critique of education, Shinde exposes the ways in which women's access to knowledge and learning is restricted by patriarchal attitudes and institutional barriers. She challenges the prevailing notion that women are inherently inferior or unsuited to intellectual pursuits, asserting their right to education as a means of self-improvement and self-realization. By advocating for equal access to education for women, Shinde seeks to dismantle the systemic inequalities that perpetuate gender inequality and constrain women's opportunities for advancement.

Religious practices also come under scrutiny in Shinde's critique of patriarchy and social norms. She exposes the ways in which religious institutions and traditions are often complicit in perpetuating gender inequality, relegating women to subordinate roles and denying them equal access to religious authority and leadership. Shinde challenges the prevailing notion that women are inherently impure or spiritually inferior to men, asserting their right to full participation in religious rituals and ceremonies.

Through her critique of religious practices, Shinde calls attention to the ways in which patriarchal attitudes and interpretations of religious texts have been used to justify women's subordination and exclusion from positions of authority within religious institutions. She advocates for a more inclusive and egalitarian approach to religion, one that recognizes the inherent dignity and worth of all individuals, regardless of gender. By challenging the patriarchal norms that govern religious practices, Shinde seeks to create space for women to fully engage with and participate in their spiritual traditions, free from discrimination and prejudice.

Central to Shinde's critique of patriarchy and social norms is her insistence on the inherent dignity and agency of women. She rejects the notion that women are inherently inferior or subordinate to men, asserting their right to autonomy, agency, and self-determination. Through her writings, she seeks to empower women to challenge the oppressive structures that constrain their lives and assert their rightful place in society as equals. Shinde's critique of patriarchy and social norms remains as relevant today as it was when it was first published, serving as a powerful reminder of the ongoing struggle for gender equality and women's rights in India and beyond.

Advocacy for Women's Education

Tarabai Shinde's advocacy for women's education stands as a cornerstone of her efforts to challenge patriarchal norms and empower women to lead lives of dignity and fulfillment. Born into a Brahmin family in Maharashtra, India, in 1850, Shinde grew up in a society characterized by rigid gender roles and limited opportunities for women's advancement. However, far from accepting the status quo, she recognized the transformative potential of education in challenging existing power structures and empowering women to assert their rights and aspirations.

At the heart of Shinde's advocacy for women's education was her belief in the inherent worth and potential of every individual, regardless of gender. She rejected the notion that women were inherently inferior or unsuited to intellectual pursuits, asserting their right to education as a means of empowerment and liberation. Shinde understood that education was not only a fundamental human right but also a powerful tool for social change, enabling women to challenge prevailing norms and assert their agency and autonomy.

One of the central themes of Shinde's advocacy was her emphasis on the transformative power of education in challenging existing power structures and empowering women to assert their rights and aspirations. She recognized that access to education was the key to unlocking women's potential and enabling them to break free from the constraints of patriarchy. By providing girls and women with opportunities for intellectual and personal growth, education served as a catalyst for social change, transforming not only individual lives but also entire communities and societies.

Shinde's advocacy for women's education was grounded in a deep understanding of the systemic barriers that prevented women from accessing education and pursuing their aspirations. She recognized that societal norms and attitudes played a significant role in perpetuating gender inequality, relegating women to domestic roles and denying them opportunities for intellectual and personal growth. Through her writings and activism, Shinde sought to challenge these norms and attitudes, advocating for greater access to education for girls and women.

One of the key challenges Shinde confronted in her advocacy for women's education was the prevailing notion that women's primary role was to serve as homemakers and caregivers. In a society where women were expected to prioritize their domestic duties over their intellectual and personal development, access to education was often limited or denied altogether. Shinde recognized the need to challenge these entrenched attitudes and stereotypes, advocating for a more inclusive and equitable approach to education that recognized the inherent worth and potential of every individual, regardless of gender.

Through her writings and activism, Shinde sought to raise awareness about the importance of women's education and its transformative potential for individuals and communities. She challenged prevailing norms and attitudes that relegated women to subordinate roles within the household and society at large, advocating for greater access to education for girls and women as a means of empowerment and liberation. By providing girls and women with opportunities for intellectual and personal growth, education served as a catalyst for social change, enabling them to challenge existing power structures and assert their rights and aspirations.

Shinde's advocacy for women's education was also informed by her recognition of the intersecting oppressions faced by women based on factors such as caste, class, and religion. She understood that women from marginalized communities were doubly oppressed, facing discrimination not only on the basis of their gender but also their caste or socio-economic status. Through her writings and activism, Shinde sought to amplify the voices of these marginalized women and challenge the intersecting systems of oppression that constrained their lives.

In addition to advocating for greater access to education for girls and women, Shinde also called for reforms in the content and delivery of education to make it more relevant and empowering for women. She recognized that traditional educational systems often reinforced gender stereotypes and perpetuated inequalities, failing to adequately address the needs and aspirations of girls and women. Through her writings and activism, Shinde advocated for curriculum reforms that promoted gender equality and challenged prevailing norms and attitudes about women's roles and capabilities.

Central to Shinde's vision of women's education was the idea of education as a tool for personal and collective empowerment. She believed that education had the power to transform not only individual lives but also entire communities and societies, enabling women to challenge existing power structures and assert their rights and aspirations. By providing girls and women with opportunities for intellectual and personal growth, education served as a catalyst for social change, empowering women to participate fully in the economic, political, and social life of their communities.

In conclusion, Tarabai Shinde's advocacy for women's education was rooted in a deep commitment to gender equality and social justice. She recognized the transformative potential of education in challenging existing power structures and empowering women to assert their rights and aspirations. Through her writings and activism, Shinde sought to raise awareness about the importance of women's education and its transformative potential for individuals and communities. By providing girls and women with opportunities for intellectual and personal growth, education served as a catalyst for social change, enabling them to challenge existing norms and attitudes and assert their agency and autonomy. Shinde's advocacy continues to inspire generations of feminists and social reformers, reminding us of the importance of education as a tool for empowerment and liberation.

Legacy and Impact

Tarabai Shinde's enduring legacy as a pioneering feminist thinker and social reformer continues to resonate in the annals of Indian feminist history. Through her groundbreaking writings and fearless activism, she left an indelible mark on the women's movement in India and beyond, inspiring generations of feminists and social reformers to challenge patriarchal norms and advocate for gender equality.

At the heart of Shinde's legacy is her seminal work, "Stri Purush Tulana" (A Comparison Between Women and Men), published in 1882. This groundbreaking essay remains a foundational text in feminist literature, offering a scathing critique of patriarchy and the oppressive social norms that perpetuate gender inequality in Indian society. Shinde's boldness in addressing taboo subjects and her unwavering commitment to women's rights challenged prevailing attitudes and inspired readers to question the status quo.

"Stri Purush Tulana" continues to be studied and analyzed by scholars and activists alike, its insights and arguments serving as a rallying cry for gender justice and social change. Shinde's meticulous deconstruction of prevailing myths and stereotypes about women's inferiority laid the groundwork for future generations of feminists to challenge patriarchal norms and advocate for gender equality. Her insistence on the inherent dignity and agency of women remains as relevant today as it was when the essay was first published, serving as a powerful reminder of the ongoing struggle for women's rights and liberation.

In addition to her writings, Shinde's activism also had a profound impact on the women's movement in India. She was unafraid to confront entrenched power structures and challenge the status quo, even at great personal risk. Through public lectures, pamphlets, and grassroots organizing, Shinde sought to mobilize women from all walks of life to demand their rightful place in society and assert their agency and autonomy. Her courage and resilience in the face of adversity continue to inspire feminists and activists to this day, reminding us of the power of individual agency and collective action in the pursuit of social justice.

Shinde's advocacy for women's rights paved the way for future generations of women to assert their autonomy and demand justice. Her boldness in addressing taboo subjects and her unwavering commitment to women's empowerment challenged prevailing attitudes and inspired readers to question the status quo. By providing a powerful critique of patriarchy and the oppressive social norms that perpetuate gender inequality, Shinde helped to lay the groundwork for a more just and equitable society, where all individuals are afforded the opportunity to realize their full potential, regardless of gender.

Shinde's legacy extends far beyond the confines of her own time and place, inspiring feminists and social reformers around the world to continue the fight for gender equality and social justice. Her courage and resilience in the face of adversity serve as a beacon of hope and inspiration for future generations, reminding us of the transformative power of individual agency and collective action in the pursuit of a more just and equitable world. As we reflect on her remarkable life and contributions, we are reminded of the enduring impact that one individual can have on the course of history, and the profound responsibility we all share to work towards a better future for generations to come.

Contemporary Relevance

Despite being written over a century ago, Tarabai Shinde's writings remain strikingly relevant in today's context. The issues she raised – including gender inequality, women's education, and patriarchal oppression – continue to resonate with contemporary feminist movements and struggles for women's rights around the world. Shinde's advocacy for women's autonomy and empowerment serves as a timeless reminder of the ongoing struggle for gender justice and equality.

In an era marked by growing awareness of gender inequality and discrimination, Shinde's critique of patriarchal norms and social injustices remains as relevant as ever. Despite significant progress in recent decades, women continue to face systemic barriers to equality and opportunity in virtually every aspect of life. From the gender pay gap to reproductive rights, from political representation to gender-based violence, the challenges confronting women today bear striking similarities to those highlighted by Shinde over a century ago.

One of the central themes of Shinde's writings is her critique of patriarchal oppression and the ways in which it manifests in various spheres of life. She exposes the double standards and hypocrisy inherent in the treatment of women, challenging prevailing norms and conventions that relegate them to subordinate roles within the household and society at large. Shinde's insistence on women's autonomy and agency remains a powerful rallying cry for contemporary feminist movements, which continue to challenge the systemic inequalities that perpetuate gender-based discrimination and violence.

Shinde's advocacy for women's education also resonates strongly with contemporary efforts to promote gender equality and empower women through education. Despite significant progress in recent decades, millions of girls around the world still lack access to quality education, perpetuating cycles of poverty and marginalization. Shinde recognized the transformative potential of education in challenging existing power structures and empowering women to assert their rights and aspirations. Her call for greater access to education for girls and women serves as a powerful reminder of the importance of investing in girls' education as a means of advancing gender equality and promoting sustainable development.

In addition to her critique of patriarchal norms and advocacy for women's education, Shinde also addressed issues related to gender-based violence and discrimination. She condemned the pervasive discrimination faced by women in various spheres of life, including marriage, employment, and access to justice. Shinde's writings on these topics remain relevant today, as women around the world continue to experience high rates of gender-based violence and discrimination in both public and private spheres. Her call for greater awareness and action to address these issues echoes the sentiments of contemporary feminist movements, which continue to advocate for legislative reforms, public awareness campaigns, and support services for survivors of gender-based violence.

Shinde's advocacy for women's autonomy and empowerment also speaks to contemporary debates surrounding reproductive rights and bodily autonomy. She recognized that women's ability to control their own bodies and make decisions about their reproductive health is fundamental to their autonomy and well-being. Shinde's writings on these topics remain relevant today, as women around the world continue to fight for access to safe and legal abortion, contraception, and reproductive healthcare services. Her call for greater recognition of women's reproductive rights and bodily autonomy resonates with contemporary feminist movements, which continue to advocate for laws and policies that respect and protect women's rights in these areas.

In addition to her advocacy for women's rights, Shinde's writings also offer insights into the intersectional nature of oppression and the ways in which gender intersects with other forms of discrimination, such as race, class, and sexuality. She recognized that women from marginalized communities face compounded forms of oppression, as they navigate intersecting systems of discrimination based on multiple axes of identity. Shinde's writings on these topics remain relevant today, as feminist movements increasingly prioritize intersectional approaches to addressing gender inequality and advancing social justice. Her call for solidarity across diverse communities and struggles echoes the sentiments of contemporary feminist movements, which continue to strive for inclusive and intersectional approaches to activism and advocacy.

Shinde's legacy serves as a testament to the enduring power of feminist thought and activism in challenging patriarchal norms and promoting gender equality. Her writings continue to inspire generations of feminists and social justice advocates to challenge the status quo and work towards a more just and equitable world for all. In an era marked by growing awareness of gender inequality and discrimination, Shinde's advocacy for women's autonomy and empowerment remains as relevant as ever, serving as a beacon of hope and inspiration for contemporary feminist movements around the world.

Conclusion

Tarabai Shinde was a visionary pioneer whose writings activism challenged the status quo and paved the way for women's rights in India. Her bold critique of patriarchy, advocacy for women's education, and unwavering commitment to gender equality continue to inspire feminists and social reformers today. As we reflect on her legacy, we are reminded of the enduring relevance of her message and the ongoing struggle for justice and equality for women everywhere. Tarabai Shinde's contributions to the women's movement serve as a beacon of hope and inspiration for future generations, reminding us of the transformative power of feminist thought and action.

3. 4 - Mahatma Phule

Mahatma Phule, also known as Jyotirao Phule, was a visionary social reformer, educator, and activist who played a pivotal role in challenging caste-based discrimination and advocating for the rights of marginalized communities in 19th century India. Born in 1827 in Maharashtra, India, Phule dedicated his life to fighting against social injustices and empowering the oppressed through education and social reform. His pioneering efforts laid the foundation for the Dalit and women's empowerment movements in India and continue to inspire social change to this day. This essay delves into the life, contributions, and enduring legacy of Mahatma Phule, highlighting his profound impact on Indian society.

Early Life and Education:

Mahatma Phule, born into a family belonging to the Mali caste, faced the harsh realities of social discrimination and marginalization from an early age. The Mali community, considered a lower-caste group in the rigid caste hierarchy of colonial India, confronted systemic barriers that limited their opportunities for advancement and relegated them to the margins of society. Despite these formidable obstacles, Phule's early experiences instilled in him a deep sense of resilience and determination to challenge the status quo and pursue education as a means of empowerment.

Phule's journey towards education began with his enrollment in a local missionary school, where he received primary education. This initial exposure to formal schooling laid the groundwork for his lifelong commitment to learning and intellectual growth. Despite the limited resources and opportunities available to him as a member of a marginalized community, Phule embraced education as a tool for personal and social transformation, recognizing its power to liberate individuals from the shackles of ignorance and oppression.

As Phule progressed through his schooling, he encountered firsthand the pervasive inequalities and injustices that permeated Indian society. The rigid caste system, which relegated certain groups to the lowest rungs of the social hierarchy based on birth, served as a formidable barrier to social mobility and advancement for millions of Indians. Phule's own experiences of discrimination and marginalization fueled his determination to challenge the entrenched power structures that perpetuated caste-based oppression and exploitation.

Despite the formidable obstacles he faced, Phule remained undeterred in his pursuit of knowledge and enlightenment. He sought out opportunities for self-improvement and intellectual growth, devouring books and engaging in discussions with like-minded individuals who shared his commitment to social justice and equality. Through his voracious appetite for learning and his unwavering dedication to the pursuit of knowledge, Phule emerged as a formidable intellectual force and a tireless advocate for the rights and dignity of marginalized communities.

Phule's early experiences of social marginalization and discrimination fueled his passion for education as a means of empowerment and liberation. He recognized that education had the power to transform not only individual lives but also entire communities and societies, enabling marginalized groups to challenge prevailing norms and assert their rights and aspirations. Phule's own journey from the margins of society to the forefront of the struggle for social justice serves as a powerful testament to the transformative potential of education in overcoming systemic barriers and effecting positive change.

In addition to his formal education, Phule was also deeply influenced by the teachings of social reformers and thinkers who challenged prevailing norms and advocated for social equality and justice. He was particularly inspired by the ideas of Western philosophers such as Thomas Paine and John Stuart Mill, whose writings on liberty, equality, and social reform resonated deeply with his own vision of a more just and equitable society. Phule's engagement with these ideas further fueled his commitment to the cause of social reform and his determination to challenge the entrenched power structures that perpetuated caste-based oppression and exploitation.

Phule's early education and intellectual development laid the foundation for his lifelong commitment to social reform and advocacy for the rights of marginalized communities. His experiences of discrimination and marginalization as a member of the Mali caste fueled his passion for education as a means of empowerment and liberation, inspiring him to challenge the entrenched power structures that perpetuated caste-based oppression and exploitation. Phule's journey from the margins of society to the forefront of the struggle for social justice serves as a powerful testament to the transformative potential of education in overcoming systemic barriers and effecting positive change.

Awakening to Social Injustice

Mahatma Phule's journey towards becoming a pioneering social reformer and advocate for social justice was deeply rooted in his experiences of caste-based discrimination and social inequality during his formative years. Born into the Mali caste, which occupied a low position in the rigid caste hierarchy of colonial India, Phule witnessed firsthand the systemic injustices and inequalities that pervaded Indian society. From a young age, he was confronted with the harsh realities of caste-based oppression and exploitation, which left a lasting impression on his worldview and ignited his passion for social reform.

Growing up in the village of Katgun, Phule was exposed to the stark inequalities that defined life in colonial India. As a member of the Mali community, he experienced firsthand the social stigma and discrimination associated with belonging to a lower-caste group. From being denied access to public spaces and resources to facing verbal abuse and physical violence, Phule and his community bore the brunt of caste-based discrimination on a daily basis. These early experiences of marginalization and injustice left an indelible mark on Phule's consciousness and fueled his determination to challenge the existing social order.

Phule's awakening to social injustice was further catalyzed by his observations of the plight of women in Indian society. As he witnessed the oppression and exploitation faced by women, particularly those from lower-caste communities, Phule became acutely aware of the intersecting forms of discrimination and inequality that shaped their lives. From the practice of child marriage to the denial of education and economic opportunities, women faced multiple barriers to their autonomy and well-being, perpetuated by patriarchal norms and social hierarchies. Phule's recognition of the interconnectedness of caste and gender-based oppression would later inform his advocacy for the rights and dignity of marginalized communities.

Phule's experiences of social injustice and oppression during his formative years served as a catalyst for his awakening to the broader social and political realities of colonial India. As he witnessed the entrenched power structures that perpetuated caste-based oppression and exploitation, Phule was compelled to challenge the existing social order and work towards creating a more equitable and just society. His experiences of marginalization and discrimination fueled his passion for social reform and his commitment to the cause of social justice, setting him on a path towards becoming one of India's most influential social reformers.

Central to Phule's awakening to social injustice was his recognition of the systemic nature of oppression and exploitation in Indian society. He understood that caste-based discrimination and social inequality were not merely individual acts of prejudice or bigotry, but rather deeply entrenched systems of power and privilege that served to maintain the dominance of certain groups at the expense of others. Phule's analysis of social injustice went beyond surface-level manifestations of discrimination to uncover the underlying structures of power and domination that perpetuated inequality and injustice.

Phule's awakening to social injustice was also informed by his engagement with the teachings of social reformers and thinkers who challenged prevailing norms and advocated for social equality and justice. He was deeply influenced by the ideas of Western philosophers such as Thomas Paine and John Stuart Mill, whose writings on liberty, equality, and social reform resonated deeply with his own vision of a more just and equitable society. Phule's engagement with these ideas further fueled his commitment to the cause of social reform and his determination to challenge the entrenched power structures that perpetuated caste-based oppression and exploitation.

Phule's awakening to social injustice was not merely a personal realization but also a call to action. He understood that challenging the status quo would require collective efforts and organized resistance against the forces of oppression and exploitation. As he witnessed the suffering and injustice faced by marginalized communities, Phule became increasingly convinced of the need for social reform and political action to address the root causes of inequality and injustice. His awakening to social injustice marked the beginning of his lifelong commitment to the cause of social justice and his tireless advocacy for the rights and dignity of marginalized communities.

In conclusion, Mahatma Phule's awakening to social injustice was deeply rooted in his experiences of caste-based discrimination and social inequality during his formative years. Witnessing the oppression and exploitation faced by lower-caste communities and women in Indian society, Phule was compelled to challenge the existing social order and work towards creating a more equitable and just society. His recognition of the systemic nature of oppression and exploitation, coupled with his engagement with the teachings of social reformers and thinkers, fueled his passion for social reform and his commitment to the cause of social justice. Phule's awakening to social injustice marked the beginning of his transformative journey towards becoming one of India's most influential social reformers and advocates for the rights and dignity of marginalized communities.

Establishment of Educational Institutions

Mahatma Phule, recognizing the transformative power of education, embarked on a pioneering journey to establish educational institutions that would provide opportunities for marginalized communities, particularly girls, to access formal schooling. His commitment to education as a means of empowerment and social transformation led him to found the first school for girls from marginalized communities in Pune in 1848, known as the Native Female School.

The establishment of the Native Female School marked a significant milestone in the history of education in colonial India. At a time when access to education was largely limited to upper-caste boys, Phule's initiative aimed to challenge the prevailing norms and provide marginalized girls with the opportunity to acquire knowledge and skills that would empower them to lead lives of dignity and agency. The school represented a radical departure from the existing educational landscape, which systematically excluded girls, particularly those from lower-caste backgrounds, from accessing formal schooling.

Phule's decision to focus specifically on girls' education was informed by his recognition of the multiple forms of discrimination and oppression faced by women in Indian society. He understood that access to education was not only a fundamental human right but also a powerful tool for challenging existing power structures and empowering marginalized communities to assert their rights and aspirations. By providing girls with the opportunity to access formal schooling, Phule sought to challenge the entrenched gender norms and social hierarchies that perpetuated inequality and injustice.

The establishment of the Native Female School was met with resistance and opposition from conservative quarters of society. Phule's efforts to promote girls' education and empowerment were seen as a direct challenge to the existing social order, which upheld patriarchal norms and caste-based hierarchies. However, Phule remained steadfast in his commitment to advancing the cause of women's education, undeterred by the obstacles and obstacles he encountered along the way.

Despite facing resistance and opposition, Phule's commitment to girls' education remained unwavering. He understood the transformative potential of education in challenging existing power structures and empowering marginalized communities to assert their rights and aspirations. The Native Female School served as a beacon of hope for girls from marginalized backgrounds, providing them with opportunities for intellectual and personal growth that were previously denied to them.

Phule's vision for education extended beyond the confines of the classroom. He understood that true empowerment required not only access to formal schooling but also opportunities for holistic development and self-actualization. In addition to academic instruction, the Native Female School provided girls with practical skills and vocational training that would enable them to pursue gainful employment and contribute to their families and communities. Phule's holistic approach to education reflected his commitment to addressing the multifaceted challenges facing marginalized communities and empowering individuals to lead lives of dignity and agency.

The establishment of the Native Female School represented a radical departure from the prevailing norms and attitudes towards girls' education in colonial India. By providing girls from marginalized communities with access to formal schooling, Phule challenged the entrenched gender norms and social hierarchies that relegated women to subordinate roles within the household and society at large. The school served as a powerful symbol of resistance and empowerment, inspiring generations of feminists and social reformers to continue the struggle for gender equality and social justice.

Phule's commitment to education as a means of empowerment and social transformation extended beyond the establishment of the Native Female School. He recognized the importance of creating a network of educational institutions that would provide opportunities for marginalized communities, particularly girls, to access formal schooling. In addition to the Native Female School, Phule founded several other educational institutions, including the Deccan Education Society, which aimed to provide quality education to students from all backgrounds.

The establishment of the Deccan Education Society represented a significant expansion of Phule's educational vision. Through this institution, he sought to create a comprehensive system of education that would cater to the diverse needs and aspirations of students from marginalized communities. The society established schools, colleges, and vocational training centers, offering a wide range of educational programs and opportunities for intellectual and personal growth.

Phule's efforts to establish educational institutions were motivated by his belief in the transformative power of education to challenge existing power structures and empower marginalized communities. He understood that access to education was not only a fundamental human right but also a powerful tool for social change. By providing girls and boys from marginalized backgrounds with access to formal schooling, Phule sought to challenge the entrenched inequalities and injustices that pervaded Indian society.

In addition to his efforts to establish educational institutions, Phule also advocated for reforms in the content and delivery of education to make it more relevant and empowering for marginalized communities. He recognized that traditional educational systems often reinforced gender norms and perpetuated inequalities, particularly for girls from lower-caste backgrounds. Phule called for curriculum reforms that promoted gender equality and challenged prevailing norms and attitudes about women's roles and capabilities.

Phule's legacy in the field of education continues to inspire generations of educators and social reformers to this day. His pioneering efforts to establish educational institutions for marginalized communities, particularly girls, laid the groundwork for the expansion of access to formal schooling in colonial India. The Native Female School and the Deccan Education Society served as powerful symbols of resistance and empowerment, challenging prevailing norms and attitudes towards girls' education and paving the way for future generations to pursue their aspirations without fear or discrimination.

Critique of Caste-Based Oppression

Mahatma Phule's advocacy extended far beyond the realm of education to encompass a broader critique of caste-based oppression and social hierarchy in Indian society. His seminal work "Gulamgiri" (Slavery), published in 1873, stands as a powerful indictment of the oppressive nature of the caste system and a call to action for the annihilation of caste-based discrimination. In "Gulamgiri, " Phule exposes the entrenched inequalities and injustices perpetuated by the upper-caste Brahmins and advocates for the rights and dignity of Dalits (formerly known as untouchables) and other marginalized communities.

At the heart of Phule's critique of caste-based oppression is his recognition of the deeply entrenched power structures that have perpetuated social inequality and exploitation for centuries. He argues that the caste system, which divides society into rigid hierarchies based on birth, is inherently unjust and oppressive, denying individuals the opportunity to realize their full potential and relegating certain groups to a lifetime of discrimination and marginalization. Phule's analysis of caste-based oppression challenges prevailing narratives that seek to justify and legitimize the status quo, instead exposing the systemic injustices that pervade Indian society.

Phule's critique of caste-based oppression is grounded in his commitment to social justice and equality. He argues that the upper-caste Brahmins, who have historically held positions of power and privilege within the caste system, have systematically exploited and marginalized lower-caste communities for their own benefit. From the imposition of social and religious restrictions to the denial of basic human rights and dignity, Phule exposes the myriad ways in which caste-based oppression manifests in everyday life, perpetuating cycles of poverty, discrimination, and exploitation.

In "Gulamgiri, " Phule challenges the prevailing narratives that seek to justify and perpetuate caste-based discrimination. He argues that the caste system is not based on merit or inherent superiority but rather on arbitrary notions of purity and pollution that serve to maintain the dominance of certain groups at the expense of others. Phule's critique of caste-based oppression seeks to dismantle the ideological foundations of the caste system and expose its inherent injustice and inhumanity.

One of the central themes of "Gulamgiri" is Phule's advocacy for the rights and dignity of Dalits and other marginalized communities. He argues that the caste system not only denies individuals the opportunity to realize their full potential but also perpetuates cycles of intergenerational poverty and exploitation. Phule calls for the annihilation of caste-based discrimination and the establishment of a more just and equitable society in which all individuals are afforded equal rights and opportunities, regardless of their caste or social status.

Phule's critique of caste-based oppression is informed by his own experiences of social marginalization and discrimination as a member of the Mali caste. From an early age, he witnessed firsthand the pervasive inequalities and injustices that permeated Indian society,

fueling his determination to challenge the status quo and work towards creating a more just and equitable society. Phule's experiences of caste-based oppression served as a catalyst for his advocacy for social reform and his commitment to the cause of social justice and equality.

In addition to his critique of caste-based oppression, Phule also challenged prevailing notions of gender inequality and advocated for the rights and dignity of women in Indian society. He recognized that patriarchy and caste-based oppression were interconnected systems of power and privilege that served to marginalize and exploit women from lower-caste backgrounds. Phule's advocacy for gender equality and women's rights was rooted in his belief in the inherent dignity and worth of all individuals, regardless of their gender or social status.

Phule's critique of caste-based oppression continues to resonate with contemporary struggles for social justice and equality in India and beyond. Despite significant progress in recent decades, caste-based discrimination remains a pervasive and deeply entrenched problem in Indian society, perpetuating cycles of poverty, discrimination, and exploitation for millions of individuals. Phule's advocacy for the annihilation of caste-based discrimination and the establishment of a more just and equitable society serves as a powerful reminder of the ongoing struggle for social justice and equality.

In conclusion, Mahatma Phule's critique of caste-based oppression in "Gulamgiri" stands as a powerful indictment of the entrenched inequalities and injustices perpetuated by the caste system in Indian society. His advocacy for the rights and dignity of Dalits and other marginalized communities challenges prevailing narratives that seek to justify and perpetuate caste-based discrimination, instead calling for the annihilation of caste-based oppression and the establishment of a more just and equitable society. Phule's critique of caste-based oppression continues to resonate with contemporary struggles for social justice and equality, serving as a powerful reminder of the

ongoing struggle to dismantle systems of oppression and create a world in which all individuals are afforded equal rights and opportunities, regardless of their caste or social status.

Emancipation of Women

Mahatma Phule's advocacy for the emancipation of women stands as a cornerstone of his social reform efforts. In a society where women were relegated to subordinate roles and denied access to education and autonomy, Phule recognized the urgent need to challenge patriarchal norms and practices in order to achieve gender equality and social justice. His tireless advocacy for women's rights paved the way for significant advancements in the status and empowerment of women in Indian society.

At a time when women's voices were often silenced and their contributions overlooked, Phule emerged as a staunch champion for women's rights and gender equality. He believed that the empowerment of women was essential for social progress and worked tirelessly to challenge the prevailing norms and practices that perpetuated their subordination and exploitation. Phule's advocacy for women's rights was grounded in his belief in the inherent dignity and worth of all individuals, regardless of their gender or social status.

Phule's wife, Savitribai Phule, played a pivotal role in his social reform activities and became one of the first female educators in India. Together, they established schools for girls and women, providing them with opportunities for education and self-improvement. The establishment of these schools marked a significant departure from prevailing norms and practices, which relegated women to domestic roles and denied them access to formal schooling.

Phule recognized the transformative power of education in challenging existing power structures and empowering marginalized communities. He understood that access to education was not only a fundamental human right but also a powerful tool for challenging patriarchal norms and practices. By providing girls and women with access to formal schooling, Phule sought to break the cycle of

ignorance and oppression that perpetuated their subordination and exploitation.

The schools established by Phule and Savitribai provided girls and women with opportunities for intellectual and personal growth that were previously denied to them. Through academic instruction, practical skills training, and vocational education, they sought to equip women with the knowledge and skills needed to assert their rights and aspirations in a patriarchal society. The schools also served as spaces of empowerment and solidarity, where women could come together to support one another and advocate for their rights.

Phule's advocacy for women's rights extended beyond education to encompass broader social and political reforms aimed at achieving gender equality and justice. He challenged prevailing norms and practices that relegated women to subordinate roles within the household and society at large, advocating for their right to autonomy, agency, and self-determination. Phule's vision of gender equality was grounded in his belief in the inherent equality of all individuals, regardless of their gender or social status.

One of the central tenets of Phule's advocacy for women's rights was his recognition of the interconnectedness of gender and caste-based oppression. He understood that women from marginalized communities faced compounded forms of discrimination and exploitation, as they navigated intersecting systems of oppression based on both gender and caste. Phule's advocacy for the rights and dignity of Dalit women, in particular, was informed by his recognition of the unique challenges they faced in Indian society.

Phule's advocacy for women's rights was not without its challenges and obstacles. He faced resistance and opposition from conservative quarters of society, which sought to uphold patriarchal norms and practices that relegated women to subordinate roles. However, Phule remained steadfast in his commitment to the cause of women's rights, undeterred by the obstacles and setbacks he encountered along the way.

The legacy of Phule's advocacy for women's rights continues to resonate with contemporary struggles for gender equality and social justice in India and beyond. Despite significant progress in recent decades, women continue to face systemic barriers to equality and opportunity in virtually every aspect of life. From the gender pay gap to reproductive rights, from political representation to gender-based violence, the challenges confronting women today bear striking similarities to those highlighted by Phule over a century ago.

In conclusion, Mahatma Phule's advocacy for the emancipation of women stands as a testament to his unwavering commitment to social justice and equality. His tireless efforts to challenge patriarchal norms and practices paved the way for significant advancements in the status and empowerment of women in Indian society. Phule's legacy continues to inspire generations of feminists and social reformers to challenge the status quo and work towards creating a more just, equitable, and inclusive society for all.

3. 5 - Savitribai Phule

Savitribai Phule, often referred to as the "Mother of Indian Feminism, " was a pioneering educator, social reformer, and advocate for women's rights in 19th century India. Born on January 3, 1831, in Naigaon, Maharashtra, Savitribai Phule defied societal norms and dedicated her life to promoting education and empowerment for girls and women, particularly from marginalized communities. Her unwavering commitment to social justice and gender equality laid the groundwork for significant advancements in women's education and rights in India. This essay explores the life, contributions, and enduring legacy of Savitribai Phule, highlighting her profound impact on Indian society.

Early Life and Education

Savitribai Phule, born into a Brahmin family in Maharashtra during the 19th century, came into the world at a time when girls from upper-caste backgrounds had limited access to education. However, despite the prevailing norms and restrictions imposed on women's education,

Savitribai's upbringing was marked by a spirit of curiosity and a thirst for knowledge. Her parents recognized the importance of education and instilled in her a love for learning from an early age.

Growing up in a society characterized by rigid gender roles and patriarchal norms, Savitribai faced numerous challenges and obstacles on her path to education. However, she was fortunate to have a supportive husband, Jyotirao Phule, who shared her belief in the transformative power of education and encouraged her to pursue her academic aspirations. Under his guidance, Savitribai embarked on a journey of self-discovery and intellectual growth that would ultimately shape her identity as a pioneering educator and social reformer.

Despite the adversity and discrimination she faced, Savitribai remained determined to pursue her education and acquire knowledge that would enable her to make a meaningful contribution to society. With Jyotirao's support, she began her formal education, learning to read and write in Marathi and English. These foundational skills laid the groundwork for her future activism and advocacy for women's rights and social reform.

Savitribai's education was not limited to formal schooling alone; she also engaged in self-directed learning and intellectual exploration, devouring books and literature on a wide range of subjects. Her voracious appetite for knowledge and her passion for learning enabled her to develop a deep understanding of the social and political issues of her time, including caste-based oppression, gender inequality, and social injustice.

As Savitribai continued her education under Jyotirao's guidance, she became increasingly aware of the systemic barriers and inequalities that pervaded Indian society, particularly for women and marginalized communities. She witnessed firsthand the pervasive discrimination and oppression faced by women from lower-caste backgrounds, who were denied access to education and subjected to various forms of social and economic exploitation.

Savitribai's experiences of social injustice and discrimination fueled her determination to challenge the status quo and work towards creating a more just and equitable society. She understood that education was not only a means of personal empowerment but also a powerful tool for social transformation. With Jyotirao's encouragement, she embarked on a mission to empower women and marginalized communities through education and advocacy.

Savitribai's journey as an educator and social reformer was marked by resilience, courage, and a deep sense of commitment to the cause of women's rights. Despite facing hostility and opposition from conservative quarters of society, she remained steadfast in her dedication to advancing the cause of education and social justice. Her unwavering belief in the inherent dignity and worth of every individual, regardless of gender or social status, guided her work and inspired others to join her in the struggle for equality and liberation.

In addition to her work as an educator, Savitribai also played a pivotal role in the establishment of schools for girls and women from marginalized communities. Alongside Jyotirao, she founded the first school for girls in Pune in 1848, breaking new ground in the field of women's education in colonial India. The establishment of these schools provided girls and women with opportunities for education and self-improvement that were previously denied to them, empowering them to assert their rights and aspirations in a patriarchal society.

Savitribai's dedication to the cause of women's education and social reform extended beyond the confines of the classroom. She was actively involved in various social and political movements aimed at challenging prevailing norms and practices that perpetuated gender inequality and social injustice. From advocating for widow remarriage to campaigning against child marriage and caste-based discrimination, Savitribai worked tirelessly to address the root causes of social inequality and oppression.

Savitribai's legacy as a pioneering educator and social reformer continues to inspire generations of feminists and social activists in India and beyond. Her unwavering commitment to the cause of women's rights and social justice serves as a powerful reminder of the transformative power of education and activism in challenging oppression and effecting positive change. Through her courage, resilience, and dedication, Savitribai Phule blazed a trail for future generations of women to follow, leaving behind a legacy that continues to shape the struggle for equality and liberation to this day.

Pioneering Efforts in Women's Education

Savitribai Phule stands as a trailblazer in the realm of women's education in India, with her pioneering efforts leaving an indelible mark on the landscape of social reform and gender equality. Her most significant contribution to Indian society was her relentless advocacy for education for girls and women, a cause she championed alongside her husband, Jyotirao Phule. Together, they embarked on a journey to establish the first girls' school in Pune in 1848, an endeavor that would revolutionize access to education for women and challenge entrenched societal norms that relegated them to subordinate roles.

The founding of the first girls' school in Pune marked a watershed moment in the history of women's education in India. Prior to this, formal education for girls was virtually non-existent, with prevailing attitudes and customs dictating that women's primary role was confined to the domestic sphere. Savitribai and Jyotirao Phule recognized the urgent need to challenge these norms and provide girls with access to education, understanding that it was the key to unlocking their potential and empowering them to lead independent and fulfilling lives.

The establishment of the girls' school in Pune represented a radical departure from prevailing norms and practices that systematically excluded girls from accessing formal education. Savitribai and Jyotirao Phule welcomed girls from all castes and backgrounds, creating an inclusive and welcoming environment where they could pursue their educational aspirations free from discrimination and prejudice. The school served as a beacon of hope for girls who had previously been denied access to education, providing them with opportunities for intellectual and personal growth that were previously unimaginable.

Savitribai's commitment to women's education was grounded in her belief in the inherent dignity and worth of every individual, regardless of gender or social status. She understood that education was not only a means of personal empowerment but also a powerful tool for social transformation. By providing girls with access to education, Savitribai sought to challenge entrenched patriarchal norms and practices that perpetuated gender inequality and oppression, paving the way for a more just and equitable society.

The establishment of the girls' school in Pune was met with resistance and opposition from conservative quarters of society, who viewed women's education as a threat to traditional gender roles and social hierarchies. However, Savitribai and Jyotirao Phule remained steadfast in their commitment to the cause of women's education, undeterred by the obstacles and challenges they faced along the way. Their unwavering determination and resilience served as a source of inspiration for generations of feminists and social reformers to come.

The girls' school in Pune provided a comprehensive education that encompassed a wide range of subjects, including language, mathematics, science, and social studies. In addition to academic instruction, the school also offered practical skills training and vocational education, equipping girls with the knowledge and skills needed to navigate the challenges of everyday life and pursue their aspirations with confidence and determination. Savitribai played a central role in the day-to-day operations of the school, serving as a teacher and mentor to the girls in her care.

Savitribai's dedication to the cause of women's education extended beyond the confines of the classroom. She was actively involved in various social and political movements aimed at challenging prevailing norms and practices that perpetuated gender inequality and social injustice. From advocating for widow remarriage to campaigning against child marriage and caste-based discrimination, Savitribai worked tirelessly to address the root causes of social inequality and oppression.

The impact of Savitribai's pioneering efforts in women's education reverberated far beyond the walls of the girls' school in Pune. Her advocacy for women's rights and gender equality inspired a wave of social reform movements across India, sparking a renewed interest in the importance of education as a tool for empowerment and social transformation. The establishment of girls' schools became increasingly common, with communities recognizing the value of providing girls with access to education and the opportunities it afforded them.

Savitribai's legacy as a pioneering educator and social reformer continues to inspire generations of feminists and social activists in India and beyond. Her unwavering commitment to the cause of women's education and social justice serves as a powerful reminder of the transformative power of education and activism in challenging oppression and effecting positive change. Through her courage, resilience, and dedication, Savitribai Phule blazed a trail for future generations of women to follow, leaving behind a legacy that continues to shape the struggle for equality and liberation to this day.

Advocacy for Women's Rights

Savitribai Phule emerged as a trailblazing advocate for women's rights in 19th-century India, using her voice and activism to challenge the entrenched patriarchal norms and practices that oppressed women and denied them their basic rights and freedoms. At a time when women's voices were often silenced and their rights denied, Savitribai fearlessly spoke out against social injustices such as child marriage, female infanticide, and the practice of purdah (seclusion of women). Through her writings and public speeches, she called attention to the plight of women in Indian society and demanded equality, dignity, and autonomy for all women.

Born into a Brahmin family in Maharashtra during a period marked by rigid gender roles and social hierarchies, Savitribai was acutely aware of the injustices faced by women from all castes and backgrounds. Despite her privileged upbringing, she recognized the systemic barriers and discrimination that prevented women from accessing education, pursuing their aspirations, and asserting their rights. Determined to challenge the status quo, Savitribai devoted her life to advocating for women's rights and social reform.

One of Savitribai's central concerns was the practice of child marriage, which condemned young girls to a lifetime of servitude and oppression. She vehemently opposed this practice, arguing that it deprived girls of their childhood, education, and autonomy. Through her writings and public speeches, Savitribai raised awareness about the detrimental effects of child marriage on girls' physical and mental well-being, as well as its contribution to perpetuating cycles of poverty and inequality. She called for legislative reforms to abolish child marriage and protect the rights of girls to pursue their education and aspirations freely.

In addition to her advocacy against child marriage, Savitribai also spoke out against female infanticide, a practice that was prevalent in certain communities and perpetuated by deeply entrenched patriarchal norms. She denounced the killing of female infants as a heinous crime against humanity and a violation of the rights and dignity of women. Through her activism, Savitribai sought to challenge the cultural attitudes and beliefs that devalued the lives of girls and perpetuated gender-based violence and discrimination. She called for greater awareness and accountability to address the root causes of female infanticide and ensure the protection and welfare of all children, regardless of their gender.

Another key aspect of Savitribai's advocacy for women's rights was her opposition to the practice of purdah, which enforced the seclusion and confinement of women within the domestic sphere. She viewed purdah as a symbol of women's oppression and subjugation, denying them the freedom to participate fully in public life, pursue education and employment, and exercise autonomy over their bodies and lives. Savitribai challenged the social norms and customs that enforced purdah, advocating for women's right to freedom of movement, expression, and choice. She argued that women should be treated as equal partners in society and afforded the same rights and opportunities as men.

Savitribai's advocacy for women's rights was rooted in her belief in the inherent dignity and worth of every individual, regardless of their gender or social status. She understood that the liberation of women was intrinsically linked to the broader struggle for social justice and equality. Through her activism, she sought to dismantle the patriarchal structures and systems of oppression that confined women to subordinate roles and denied them their basic rights and freedoms. She called for a radical transformation of society that would recognize and respect the humanity and agency of women in all spheres of life.

Despite facing resistance and opposition from conservative quarters of society, Savitribai remained steadfast in her commitment to the cause of women's rights. She refused to be silenced or intimidated by threats and violence, continuing to speak out against injustice and advocate for equality and dignity for all women. Her courage, resilience, and determination served as a source of inspiration for generations of feminists and social reformers to come, inspiring them to continue the struggle for women's rights and social justice.

Savitribai's advocacy for women's rights extended beyond her public activism to encompass her personal relationships and everyday interactions. As a teacher and mentor to girls and women from marginalized communities, she provided them with encouragement, support, and guidance, empowering them to assert their rights and aspirations in a patriarchal society. Through her example, she demonstrated the importance of solidarity and sisterhood in the fight for gender equality and social justice.

In conclusion, Savitribai Phule's advocacy for women's rights stands as a testament to her unwavering commitment to social justice and equality. Through her activism, she challenged the entrenched patriarchal norms and practices that oppressed women and denied them their basic rights and freedoms. Her courage, resilience, and determination continue to inspire generations of feminists and social reformers to challenge injustice and work towards creating a more just, equitable, and inclusive society for all.

Addressing Social Issues

In addition to her work in education and women's rights, Savitribai Phule addressed a wide range of social issues affecting marginalized communities in India. She was actively involved in campaigns against caste-based discrimination, untouchability, and social inequalities. Savitribai Phule's advocacy extended to issues such as widow remarriage, which was taboo in Indian society at the time, and she worked tirelessly to challenge the stigma associated with widows and advocate for their rights.

Empowering Through Literacy

Savitribai Phule believed that education was the key to empowerment and liberation for women. She recognized that literacy was a tool for social transformation and worked tirelessly to promote literacy among women from all backgrounds. Through her efforts, countless women gained access to education and acquired the skills and knowledge needed to assert their rights, challenge oppression, and participate actively in society.

Overcoming Challenges

Savitribai Phule faced numerous challenges and obstacles in her quest for social reform and women's empowerment. She endured criticism, ostracism, and even physical attacks from conservative quarters of society that opposed her progressive ideas and actions. Despite these challenges, she remained steadfast in her commitment to social justice and continued to advocate for the rights of marginalized communities until her untimely death in 1897.

Legacy and Enduring Impact

Savitribai Phule's contributions to Indian society have left an indelible mark on the history of women's empowerment and social reform in India. Her pioneering efforts in promoting education for girls and women laid the foundation for the women's education movement in India and inspired generations of feminists and social reformers. Savitribai Phule's legacy continues to resonate in contemporary India, where her spirit of resilience, courage, and compassion serves as a guiding light for those fighting for gender equality and social justice.

Commemoration and Recognition

In recognition of her contributions to Indian society, Savitribai Phule has been commemorated and honored in various ways. Educational institutions, streets, and buildings have been named after her, and her life and work have been celebrated through books, films, and cultural events. Her birthday, January 3, is celebrated as "Savitribai Phule Jayanti" in Maharashtra and other parts of India, where tributes are paid to her pioneering efforts in advancing women's rights and education.

Conclusion

Savitribai Phule's life and work exemplify the transformative power of education, activism, and advocacy in challenging social injustices and empowering marginalized communities. Her unwavering commitment to women's rights and social reform continues to inspire individuals and movements around the world. As we reflect on her legacy, let us honor Savitribai Phule's pioneering spirit and rededicate ourselves to the ongoing struggle for gender equality, social justice, and human rights for all.

3. 6 - Dr. Babasaheb Ambedkar

Babasaheb Dr. Bhimrao Ramji Ambedkar, commonly known as Dr. B. R. Ambedkar, was a visionary leader, social reformer, jurist, and the chief architect of the Indian Constitution. Born on April 14, 1891, in the town of Mhow in present-day Madhya Pradesh, India, Ambedkar overcame immense social and economic obstacles to become one of the most influential figures in modern Indian history. His tireless advocacy for the rights of marginalized communities, particularly Dalits (formerly known as untouchables), and his relentless pursuit of social justice have left an indelible mark on Indian society. This essay explores the life, contributions, and enduring legacy of Babasaheb Ambedkar, highlighting his profound impact on the struggle for equality, dignity, and human rights.

Early Life and Education:

Babasaheb Ambedkar was born into a Dalit family belonging to the Mahar caste, which was considered one of the lowest in the rigid caste hierarchy of colonial India. Despite facing discrimination and social marginalization from a young age, Ambedkar's quest for knowledge and desire to uplift his community propelled him to pursue education against all odds. He excelled academically and earned multiple degrees, including a Bachelor's degree from Bombay University, a Master's degree from Columbia University in the United States, and a doctorate from the University of London.

Advocacy for Dalit Rights:

Throughout his life, Babasaheb Ambedkar was a fierce advocate for the rights and dignity of Dalits, who had long been subjected to social, economic, and political oppression in Indian society. He tirelessly fought against caste-based discrimination and untouchability, challenging the discriminatory practices and customs that relegated Dalits to the margins of society. Ambedkar's seminal work, "Annihilation of Caste, " published in 1936, critiqued the caste system and called for its abolition, arguing that caste hierarchy perpetuated inequality and injustice.

Leadership in the Dalit Movement

Babasaheb Ambedkar emerged as a leader of the Dalit movement in India, mobilizing Dalits to assert their rights and demand social and political equality. He founded the Independent Labour Party in 1936 to represent the interests of Dalits and other marginalized communities and advocated for their inclusion in the political process. Ambedkar's leadership and advocacy paved the way for the empowerment of Dalits and inspired generations of social justice activists in India and beyond.

Role in the Indian Independence Movement

Babasaheb Ambedkar played a significant role in the Indian independence movement, advocating for social and political reforms to address the entrenched inequalities and injustices in Indian society. He was a prominent member of the Indian National Congress and worked alongside other nationalist leaders to fight for India's independence from British colonial rule. However, Ambedkar soon realized that political independence alone would not guarantee social justice for Dalits and marginalized communities, leading him to advocate for separate representation and safeguards for Dalits in the political system.

Architect of the Indian Constitution

Babasaheb Ambedkar's most enduring contribution to Indian society came in his role as the chairman of the Drafting Committee of the Constituent Assembly of India. As the principal architect of the Indian Constitution, Ambedkar played a pivotal role in shaping the foundational document of independent India, which enshrines principles of democracy, equality, and social justice. He championed provisions for fundamental rights, affirmative action, and reservations for marginalized communities, including Scheduled Castes (Dalits) and Scheduled Tribes, in education, employment, and political representation.

Advocate for Women's Rights

Babasaheb Ambedkar was also a staunch advocate for women's rights and gender equality. He recognized the intersecting forms of oppression faced by Dalit women and worked to address their unique challenges and vulnerabilities. Ambedkar campaigned for legal reforms to improve the status of women, including laws prohibiting child marriage and ensuring inheritance rights for women. He also emphasized the importance of education and economic independence for women as pathways to empowerment and liberation from patriarchal norms and practices.

Legacy and Enduring Impact

Babasaheb Ambedkar's contributions to Indian society have had a profound and lasting impact on the struggle for social justice, equality, and human rights. His leadership in the Dalit movement, his role in the Indian independence movement, and his instrumental role in drafting the Indian Constitution have earned him widespread admiration and respect. Ambedkar's ideas and principles continue to inspire social justice movements and advocacy efforts in India and around the world, particularly among marginalized communities fighting against caste-based discrimination and oppression.

Commemoration and Recognition

Babasaheb Ambedkar's legacy is commemorated and celebrated in various ways across India. His birthday, April 14, is celebrated as "Ambedkar Jayanti" and is observed as a public holiday in several Indian states. Statues and memorials dedicated to Ambedkar can be found in cities and towns across India, symbolizing his enduring legacy as a champion of social justice and human rights. Additionally, educational institutions, scholarships, and awards have been established in his name to honor his contributions to education and social reform.

CHAPTER - 4

PROVISIONS FOR WOMEN EDUCATION

4. 1 - Constitutional Provisions and Government Strategies

India's commitment to women's education is deeply rooted in its Constitution, which provides several provisions to ensure gender equality and promote women's empowerment. These constitutional articles, along with various government strategies, aim to create an inclusive educational environment where women can access and benefit from educational opportunities. Here, we explore key constitutional provisions and government strategies focused on women's education.

4. 1. 1 - Constitutional Articles: Article 14, 15(3), 39(d), 42

Article 14: Right to Equality

Article 14 of the Indian Constitution is a cornerstone of Indian democracy, enshrining the principle of equality before the law and equal protection of the laws. This fundamental right is vital in the effort to create a society where every individual, regardless of their gender, can access equal opportunities, particularly in education. By promoting equality and prohibiting discrimination based on gender, Article 14 serves as a powerful tool to challenge and rectify inequalities in educational institutions. This article will explore the significance of Article 14, its role in promoting women's education, and the legal and social frameworks it influences.

Understanding Article 14

Article 14 of the Indian Constitution states: "The State shall not deny to any person equality before the law or the equal protection of the laws within the territory of India. " This provision embodies two key principles:

1. Equality Before the Law: This means that no individual is above the law and everyone is subject to the same laws irrespective of their status or identity.

2. Equal Protection of the Laws: This implies that the State must ensure that all individuals are treated equally and that any necessary affirmative actions are taken to achieve substantive equality.

Article 14 and Women's Education

Women's education has historically faced significant barriers due to deep-seated patriarchal norms and discriminatory practices. Article 14 plays a pivotal role in addressing these challenges by providing a constitutional guarantee against gender-based discrimination in educational settings.

1. The Right to Education Act, 2009: This Act aims to provide free and compulsory education to children aged 6 to 14 years. It emphasizes the need to eliminate gender disparities in education and ensures that girls have access to quality education.

2. The National Policy on Education, 1986 (and its subsequent revisions): This policy has consistently emphasized the importance of women's education, advocating for the removal of disparities and the promotion of gender-sensitive curricula.

3. The Supreme Court of India: Through various judgments, the Supreme Court has reinforced the principle of equality in education. Notable cases like the Vishaka v. State of Rajasthan (1997) have underscored the need to protect women's rights in all spheres, including education.

Socio-Economic Impact of Article 14 on Women's Education

1. Increasing Enrollment and Retention Rates: The enforcement of Article 14 has led to significant strides in increasing the enrollment and retention rates of girls in schools. Government schemes such as the Beti Bachao, Beti Padhao initiative have been instrumental in promoting girls' education, ensuring that they have the same opportunities as boys.

2. Scholarships and Financial Aid: Various scholarship programs aimed at encouraging girls to pursue higher education have been implemented. These initiatives are grounded in the principles of

Article 14, ensuring that financial constraints do not impede a girl's right to education. For instance, the Central Sector Scheme of Scholarship for College and University Students provides financial support to meritorious girls from economically disadvantaged backgrounds.

3. Infrastructure Development: Article 14 has also led to improvements in the educational infrastructure to support girls' education. This includes the construction of separate toilets for girls, provision of sanitary napkins, and the establishment of residential schools for girls in remote areas. Such measures are crucial in ensuring that girls do not drop out of school due to lack of basic facilities.

4. Challenges and the Way Forward: Despite the legal guarantees and significant progress made, several challenges remain in achieving complete gender parity in education.

5. Cultural and Social Barriers: Deep-rooted cultural norms and societal attitudes continue to hinder girls' education. Issues such as early marriage, preference for male children, and societal expectations around gender roles need to be addressed through continuous advocacy and awareness programs.

6. Quality of Education: While access to education has improved, the quality of education received by girls, particularly in rural areas, remains a concern. Efforts must be made to ensure that educational institutions provide quality education that empowers girls and prepares them for future opportunities.

7. Legal Enforcement and Implementation: Effective implementation of laws and policies is critical. There is a need for robust monitoring mechanisms to ensure that educational institutions adhere to the principles of Article 14. Moreover, legal literacy programs should be conducted to make women aware of their rights under Article 14, enabling them to challenge any form of discrimination.

8. Promoting Gender-Sensitive Education: To truly realize the vision of Article 14, educational curricula must be gender-sensitive. This involves integrating gender studies into the curriculum, promoting co-educational activities that challenge stereotypes, and training teachers to adopt inclusive teaching practices.

9. Role of Civil Society and NGOs: Civil society organizations and non-governmental organizations (NGOs) play a crucial role in promoting women's education and advocating for their rights. Initiatives by these organizations have led to increased awareness and grassroots-level changes that complement governmental efforts. Programs such as community-based education initiatives and advocacy campaigns against child marriage have been pivotal in driving change.

Article 14 of the Indian Constitution is not just a legal provision but a beacon of hope for millions of girls and women aspiring for a better future through education. By guaranteeing equality before the law and equal protection of the laws, it lays the foundation for a just and equitable society. The ongoing efforts to promote women's education, backed by the principles enshrined in Article 14, have led to significant progress. However, continued vigilance, effective implementation of laws, and a shift in societal attitudes are essential to overcoming the remaining barriers and ensuring that every girl in India can exercise her right to education fully and equally.

4. 1. 2 - Article 15(3): Positive Discrimination in Favor of Women

The Indian Constitution stands as a beacon of equality and justice, ensuring that all citizens are treated fairly and equitably. Among its many progressive provisions, Article 15 is particularly significant in addressing issues of discrimination. While Article 15(1) explicitly prohibits discrimination on grounds such as religion, race, caste, sex, or place of birth, Article 15(3) introduces a critical exception that allows the state to make special provisions for women and children. This clause enables the government to implement affirmative actions and policies specifically aimed at enhancing women's access to education and other opportunities. In this essay, we will explore the importance of Article 15(3), the types of measures it enables, and its impact on society.

Understanding Article 15(3)

Article 15(3) of the Indian Constitution states: "Nothing in this article shall prevent the State from making any special provision for women and children." This clause is a form of positive discrimination, which is essential in addressing systemic and historical injustices faced by women. Positive discrimination, or affirmative action, involves policies and practices that favor those who tend to suffer from discrimination, with the goal of achieving equal opportunity for all.

The inclusion of Article 15(3) in the Constitution was a recognition of the deep-rooted gender inequalities prevalent in Indian society. Historically, women in India have faced numerous barriers, including limited access to education, economic opportunities, and political participation. These inequalities were not merely social but were often institutionalized, making it difficult for women to break free from the cycle of disadvantage. The framers of the Constitution acknowledged that merely prohibiting discrimination was insufficient to bring about substantive equality. There was a need for proactive measures to uplift women and ensure they could participate fully in all spheres of life.

One of the most significant measures enabled by Article 15(3) is the provision of scholarships and financial aid specifically for girls and women. These scholarships are designed to reduce the financial barriers that prevent many girls from pursuing education. Examples include the Pragati Scholarship for Girl Students and various state-level initiatives that provide financial support to girls from economically disadvantaged backgrounds. Such scholarships have played a crucial role in increasing the enrollment and retention rates of girls in schools and colleges.

Reservation of Seats in Educational Institutions

Article 15(3) also empowers the government to reserve seats for women in educational institutions. This reservation ensures that a certain percentage of seats in schools, colleges, and universities are allocated to female students, thus promoting gender diversity in higher education. For instance, many Indian Institutes of Technology (IITs) have implemented a reservation policy to increase the number of female students in engineering programs. This policy aims to bridge the gender gap in STEM fields, which have traditionally been male-dominated.

Schemes to Reduce Dropout Rates

The government, under the purview of Article 15(3), has introduced various schemes to reduce dropout rates among female students. These schemes address the socio-economic factors that contribute to high dropout rates, such as child marriage, household responsibilities, and lack of sanitation facilities. Programs like the Kasturba Gandhi Balika Vidyalaya (KGBV) provide residential schooling facilities for girls from marginalized communities, ensuring that they can continue their education without interruption. Additionally, the provision of separate toilets for girls in schools and the distribution of sanitary napkins are measures aimed at creating a conducive environment for girls to stay in school.

Impact of Positive Discrimination on Women's Education

Positive discrimination is crucial in addressing the historical injustices faced by women. For centuries, women in India were denied the right to education and economic independence. By implementing affirmative action policies, the state is not only rectifying past wrongs but also creating a more equitable society. These measures have opened doors for millions of women, enabling them to achieve their potential and contribute to the nation's development.

Empowerment and Economic Independence

Education is a powerful tool for empowerment. By ensuring that more women have access to quality education, Article 15(3) helps in promoting economic independence among women. Educated women are better equipped to secure employment, start their businesses, and participate in economic activities. This economic empowerment has a ripple effect, leading to improved living standards for families and communities. Moreover, educated women are more likely to advocate for their rights and participate in decision-making processes, furthering gender equality.

Changing Societal Attitudes

The implementation of Article 15(3) has also contributed to changing societal attitudes towards women's education. In many parts of India, there is still a preference for educating boys over girls. However, government initiatives and affirmative action policies have raised awareness about the importance of educating girls. As more girls enroll in schools and colleges, communities begin to see the benefits of women's education, such as improved health outcomes, reduced fertility rates, and enhanced economic productivity. Over time, these changes contribute to shifting societal norms and reducing gender biases.

Challenges and Criticisms

While Article 15(3) has been instrumental in promoting women's education, it is not without its challenges and criticisms.

Implementation Gaps

One of the primary challenges is the gap between policy formulation and implementation. Despite the existence of numerous schemes and programs, their impact is often limited by inadequate implementation at the grassroots level. Issues such as corruption, lack of infrastructure, and insufficient funding hinder the effectiveness of these measures. Ensuring that policies reach the intended beneficiaries requires robust monitoring and accountability mechanisms.

Resistance to Positive Discrimination

Positive discrimination often faces resistance from various quarters. Critics argue that affirmative action policies can lead to reverse discrimination, where individuals from non-targeted groups feel disadvantaged. There is also a concern that reservations and quotas might compromise meritocracy. However, it is important to recognize that these measures are temporary and aimed at achieving long-term equality. The ultimate goal is to create a level playing field where such provisions are no longer necessary.

Balancing Affirmative Action with Merit

Balancing affirmative action with merit remains a contentious issue. While it is crucial to provide opportunities to historically disadvantaged groups, it is equally important to maintain standards of excellence in educational institutions. Policymakers must ensure that affirmative action policies do not dilute the quality of education. This can be achieved by providing additional support and resources to help beneficiaries meet the required standards rather than lowering the criteria for admission.

The Way Forward

To maximize the benefits of Article 15(3) and ensure sustainable progress in women's education, several steps need to be taken.

Strengthening Implementation

Effective implementation is key to the success of affirmative action policies. This requires adequate funding, infrastructure development, and capacity-building initiatives at the grassroots level. Local governments and educational institutions must be held accountable for the delivery of schemes and programs. Regular monitoring and evaluation can help identify gaps and areas for improvement, ensuring that policies achieve their intended outcomes.

Enhancing Awareness and Advocacy

Awareness campaigns and advocacy efforts are essential to changing societal attitudes towards women's education. Engaging with community leaders, parents, and educators can help dispel myths and stereotypes about educating girls. Additionally, highlighting success stories and role models can inspire more families to invest in their daughters' education. Collaboration with civil society organizations and NGOs can amplify these efforts and reach a wider audience.

Focus on Quality Education

While increasing access to education is crucial, ensuring the quality of education is equally important. This involves training teachers, developing gender-sensitive curricula, and creating a supportive learning environment. Special emphasis should be placed on subjects where women are underrepresented, such as STEM fields. Providing mentorship and career guidance can help female students navigate their educational and professional journeys effectively.

Inclusive Policy-Making

Policy-making should be inclusive and participatory, involving stakeholders from diverse backgrounds. Women's voices must be heard in the decision-making process to ensure that policies address their specific needs and challenges. Engaging with educators, students, parents, and community leaders can provide valuable insights and help design effective interventions.

Article 15(3) of the Indian Constitution represents a significant step towards achieving gender equality in education. By allowing the state to make special provisions for women, it acknowledges the historical and systemic disadvantages faced by women and provides a framework for addressing them. The affirmative action policies and measures enabled by this clause have made substantial progress in promoting women's education and empowerment. However, continuous efforts are needed to overcome implementation challenges, change societal attitudes, and ensure that quality education is accessible to all women. The journey towards gender equality is ongoing, and Article 15(3) remains a vital tool in this endeavor.

4. 1. 3 - Article 39(d): Equal Pay for Equal Work

Article 39(d) of the Indian Constitution is a crucial component of the Directive Principles of State Policy, which guide the state in formulating policies aimed at securing economic and social justice. This article mandates that both men and women receive equal pay for equal work, addressing economic disparities and promoting gender equality in the workforce. While the primary focus of Article 39(d) is on economic equality, its implications extend to various sectors, including education. By advocating for gender parity in the workforce, Article 39(d) underscores the importance of educating women to ensure they can compete equally in the job market and contribute significantly to the economy. This essay will explore the significance of Article 39(d), the challenges in its implementation, its broader impact on society, and the way forward in achieving true economic equality.

Understanding Article 39(d)

Article 39(d) states: "The State shall, in particular, direct its policy towards securing that there is equal pay for equal work for both men and women. " This directive principle is not enforceable by law but serves as a guiding principle for the state to ensure that policies and laws are aligned with the goals of economic justice and gender equality. The provision aims to eliminate wage disparities between men and women who perform the same work under similar conditions, thereby promoting fairness and equity in the labor market.

The inclusion of Article 39(d) in the Constitution was a response to the widespread economic inequalities and gender-based wage discrimination prevalent in India at the time of its drafting. The framers of the Constitution recognized that economic justice was fundamental to achieving social justice and that ensuring equal pay for equal work was a critical step towards eliminating gender-based economic disparities. This principle was influenced by global labor movements and international conventions advocating for gender equality in the workplace, such as the International Labour Organization's Equal Remuneration Convention of 1951.

1. Addressing Wage Disparities: The primary aim of Article 39(d) is to address and eliminate wage disparities between men and women. Wage discrimination can have far-reaching implications, including perpetuating poverty, limiting women's economic independence, and reinforcing gender inequality. By mandating equal pay for equal work, Article 39(d) seeks to ensure that women are compensated fairly for their contributions to the workforce, thereby promoting economic justice and enhancing their financial security.

2. Promoting Workforce Participation: Equal pay for equal work is essential for encouraging greater participation of women in the workforce. When women are assured of fair compensation, they are more likely to seek employment and remain in the workforce. This increased participation not only benefits women but also contributes to the overall economic growth and development of the country. A diverse and inclusive workforce is more innovative, productive, and resilient, making gender parity in employment a critical economic objective.

3. Importance of Educating Women: The principle of equal pay for equal work is intrinsically linked to the education of women. Education equips women with the skills and knowledge necessary to compete in the job market on an equal footing with men. It empowers women to pursue a wide range of career opportunities and enhances their employability. By advocating for gender parity in the workforce, Article 39(d) underscores the need to invest in women's education to ensure they can achieve economic equality.

4. Reducing Gender Stereotypes: Education plays a vital role in challenging and changing societal attitudes and stereotypes that limit women's roles to certain types of work. By providing girls with access to quality education and encouraging them to pursue careers in various fields, society can break down the barriers that contribute to occupational segregation and wage disparities. This, in turn, aligns with the goals of Article 39(d) by promoting a more inclusive and equitable labor market.

5. Legal and Institutional Barriers: Despite the clear mandate of Article 39(d), achieving equal pay for equal work remains a significant challenge in India. One of the primary obstacles is the lack of robust legal frameworks and institutional mechanisms to enforce this principle effectively. While there are laws such as the Equal Remuneration Act of 1976, enforcement is often weak, and many cases of wage discrimination go unreported or unresolved.

6. Informal Sector and Unorganized Labor: A substantial portion of India's workforce is employed in the informal sector, where labor laws are not strictly enforced, and wage disparities are rampant. Women in these sectors often face significant wage discrimination, with little recourse to legal remedies. Addressing wage disparities in the informal sector requires comprehensive policy measures and targeted interventions to protect the rights of women workers.

7. Societal Attitudes and Cultural Norms: Deep-rooted societal attitudes and cultural norms continue to perpetuate gender discrimination in the workplace. Traditional views about gender roles often result in women being undervalued and underpaid. Changing these attitudes requires sustained efforts in education, awareness campaigns, and the promotion of gender-sensitive policies at all levels of society.

Broader Impact on Society

1. Economic Growth and Development: Achieving equal pay for equal work has broader implications for economic growth and development. When women are paid fairly, their increased purchasing power can stimulate economic activity and drive demand for goods and services. Furthermore, gender equality in the workforce can lead to better decision-making and more effective utilization of human resources, contributing to overall economic efficiency and productivity.

2. Social Justice and Equity: Equal pay for equal work is a matter of social justice and equity. It recognizes the value of women's labor and ensures that they are treated with dignity and respect in the workplace. By addressing wage disparities, society moves closer to achieving true gender equality and social justice, creating a more just and equitable society for all.

3. Empowerment and Agency: Fair compensation empowers women by enhancing their financial independence and agency. When women have control over their finances, they can make decisions about their lives, health, and well-being. This empowerment extends to their families and communities, as women are more likely to invest in their children's education and health, contributing to intergenerational benefits.

Strengthening Legal Frameworks

To effectively implement Article 39(d), it is essential to strengthen the legal frameworks that support equal pay for equal work. This includes revising and updating existing laws, ensuring stricter enforcement, and establishing clear mechanisms for addressing wage discrimination. Legal reforms should also focus on extending protections to workers in the informal sector and ensuring that all women have access to legal remedies.

Enhancing Monitoring and Accountability

Effective monitoring and accountability mechanisms are crucial for ensuring compliance with equal pay provisions. This can involve regular audits of wage practices, transparent reporting by employers, and the establishment of independent bodies to investigate and resolve complaints of wage discrimination. Strengthening labor inspection systems and providing adequate resources for enforcement agencies are also necessary steps.

Promoting Gender-Sensitive Policies

Policymakers must adopt and promote gender-sensitive policies that address the root causes of wage disparities. This includes measures to support work-life balance, such as affordable childcare, parental leave, and flexible working arrangements. Additionally, efforts should be made to encourage women's participation in traditionally male-dominated fields through targeted education and training programs.

Raising Awareness and Advocacy

Raising awareness about the importance of equal pay for equal work is critical for changing societal attitudes and behaviors. Advocacy campaigns, public education programs, and collaborations with civil society organizations can help build a broad-based movement for gender equality in the workplace. Highlighting success stories and role models can inspire change and demonstrate the benefits of fair compensation.

Article 39(d) of the Indian Constitution represents a vital commitment to economic justice and gender equality. By mandating equal pay for equal work, it addresses the pervasive issue of wage discrimination and promotes a more equitable and inclusive labor market. While significant challenges remain in its implementation, the principle of equal pay for equal work has far-reaching implications for economic growth, social justice, and the empowerment of women. To realize the full potential of Article 39(d), it is essential to strengthen legal frameworks, enhance monitoring and accountability, promote gender-sensitive policies, and raise awareness about the importance of wage equality. Through concerted efforts and sustained commitment, India can move closer to achieving true economic and social justice for all its citizens.

4. 1. 4 - Article 42: Just and Humane Conditions of Work and Maternity Relief

Article 42 of the Indian Constitution is a significant component of the Directive Principles of State Policy, aiming to ensure social and economic justice for workers. This article mandates that the state should make provisions for securing just and humane conditions of work and for maternity relief. By focusing on humane work conditions and maternity benefits, Article 42 acknowledges the unique challenges faced by women, particularly in balancing education, work, and family responsibilities. By ensuring maternity relief and humane work conditions, Article 42 indirectly supports women's education and professional development, allowing them to pursue their careers without having to choose between education and family obligations.

Understanding Article 42

Article 42 states: "The State shall make provision for securing just and humane conditions of work and for maternity relief. " This directive is a reflection of the state's commitment to safeguarding the rights and welfare of workers, particularly women. Although the Directive Principles are not enforceable by law, they serve as fundamental guidelines for the governance of the country, influencing policy-making and legislation.

The inclusion of Article 42 in the Constitution was driven by the recognition of the harsh and often inhumane conditions under which many workers, especially women, were employed. During the drafting of the Constitution, India was emerging from colonial rule, where labor exploitation was rampant. The framers of the Constitution aimed to create a more equitable society by ensuring that all workers could enjoy just and humane conditions of work. The provision for maternity relief was particularly important, as it acknowledged the biological and social responsibilities of women, aiming to protect their health and well-being during and after pregnancy.

Definition and Importance

Just and humane conditions of work refer to environments where workers are treated with dignity, provided fair wages, reasonable working hours, safe working conditions, and access to necessary amenities. These conditions are crucial for maintaining the physical and mental well-being of workers, which in turn enhances productivity and job satisfaction.

Legal Framework and Policies

Several laws and policies have been enacted to ensure just and humane conditions of work in India. The Factories Act, 1948, the Minimum Wages Act, 1948, and the Occupational Safety, Health, and Working Conditions Code, 2020, are some of the key legislations that regulate working conditions. These laws set standards for working hours, minimum wages, safety measures, and welfare provisions, aiming to protect workers from exploitation and hazardous conditions.

Challenges in Implementation

Despite the legal framework, the implementation of these laws remains a challenge. Many workers, especially in the informal sector, continue to face poor working conditions. Issues such as lack of awareness, inadequate enforcement mechanisms, and resistance from employers contribute to the persistence of inhumane working conditions. Strengthening labor inspection systems, enhancing worker education, and ensuring strict enforcement of labor laws are essential steps to address these challenges.

Importance of Maternity Relief

Maternity relief is essential for protecting the health and well-being of women and their children. It allows women to take time off from work during the critical periods before and after childbirth without fear of losing their jobs or income. Maternity benefits also support women's ability to balance their roles as workers and caregivers, contributing to gender equality in the workplace.

The Maternity Benefit Act, 1961, is the primary legislation governing maternity benefits in India. This Act entitles women to paid maternity leave, job protection, and other benefits related to pregnancy and childbirth. The Act was amended in 2017 to increase the duration of paid maternity leave from 12 weeks to 26 weeks, reflecting the state's commitment to enhancing maternity relief for women workers.

Challenges in Implementation

While the legal provisions for maternity relief are robust, several challenges hinder their effective implementation. Many women, particularly those in the informal sector, do not have access to these benefits. Employers in the formal sector sometimes view maternity benefits as a financial burden, leading to discriminatory practices against women of childbearing age. Addressing these issues requires comprehensive measures, including better enforcement of existing laws, incentivizing employers to comply, and extending benefits to informal sector workers.

Linkage with Women's Education and Professional Development

1. Supporting Women's Education: By ensuring just and humane work conditions and maternity relief, Article 42 indirectly supports women's education. When women are assured of safe working environments and maternity benefits, they are more likely to pursue higher education and professional development opportunities. This security allows women to balance their educational pursuits with their family responsibilities, reducing the dropout rates and encouraging continuous learning and skill development.

2. Encouraging Career Advancement: Maternity relief and humane work conditions also play a crucial role in supporting women's career advancement. Women often face career interruptions due to pregnancy and childcare responsibilities. By providing maternity leave and ensuring job protection, Article 42 helps women to return to their careers post-childbirth without facing discrimination or setbacks. This continuity is vital for career progression and helps in closing the gender gap in leadership and higher positions in the workforce.

Broader Impact on Society

1. Economic Growth and Productivity: Ensuring just and humane work conditions and maternity relief has broader implications for economic growth and productivity. Healthy and satisfied workers are more productive and contribute positively to the economy. When women participate fully in the workforce, it leads to a more diverse and dynamic labor market, driving innovation and economic development.

2. Social Justice and Gender Equality: Article 42 promotes social justice by ensuring that all workers are treated fairly and with respect. By addressing the specific needs of women, particularly through maternity relief, the state promotes gender equality in the workplace. This not only benefits women but also fosters a more inclusive society where everyone has the opportunity to thrive.

3. Improved Health and Well-being: Humane work conditions and maternity relief significantly impact the health and well-being of workers. Safe and healthy work environments reduce the risk of work-related injuries and illnesses. Maternity benefits support the health of mothers and their children, leading to better long-term health outcomes. These factors contribute to a healthier workforce and society overall.

Challenges and Criticisms

1. Informal Sector and Unorganized Labor: One of the primary challenges in implementing Article 42 is the prevalence of informal and unorganized labor in India. A significant portion of the workforce is employed in sectors where labor laws are not strictly enforced, and workers do not have access to basic rights and benefits. Extending the protections of Article 42 to these workers requires targeted policies and interventions.

2. Financial Burden on Employers: Employers often view the provisions for humane work conditions and maternity relief as financial burdens. This perception can lead to resistance and non-compliance. Addressing this challenge requires a balanced approach that incentivizes employers to comply with the laws while ensuring that the financial implications are manageable. Government subsidies and support for small and medium enterprises can help in this regard.

3. Awareness and Education: Lack of awareness about labor rights and maternity benefits among workers is another significant challenge. Many workers are unaware of their entitlements under the law, which prevents them from claiming their rights. Educational programs and awareness campaigns are essential to inform workers about their rights and how to exercise them.

Strengthening Legal Frameworks and Enforcement

Strengthening the legal frameworks and enforcement mechanisms is crucial for the effective implementation of Article 42. This includes updating existing laws to cover emerging issues, enhancing labor inspection systems, and ensuring strict penalties for non-compliance.

Collaboration between government agencies, employers, and worker organizations can enhance the effectiveness of enforcement efforts.

1. **Extending Protections to Informal Sector Workers:** Extending the protections of Article 42 to informal sector workers requires innovative policy solutions. This could include creating social security schemes for informal workers, providing incentives for employers to formalize their workforce, and establishing community-based monitoring systems to ensure compliance with labor laws.

2. **Promoting Gender-Sensitive Work Policies:** Promoting gender-sensitive work policies is essential to address the specific needs of women in the workplace. This includes measures such as flexible working hours, provision of childcare facilities, and parental leave policies that support both mothers and fathers. Such policies can help create a more inclusive and supportive work environment for women.

3. **Raising Awareness and Education:** Raising awareness about labor rights and maternity benefits is critical for empowering workers. This can be achieved through educational programs, awareness campaigns, and collaboration with civil society organizations. Providing accessible information and resources can help workers understand their rights and how to claim them.

Article 42 of the Indian Constitution represents a significant commitment to social and economic justice for workers, particularly women. By mandating just and humane conditions of work and maternity relief, it addresses the unique challenges faced by women in balancing education, work, and family responsibilities. The provisions of Article 42 not only enhance the well-being of workers but also support women's education and professional development, contributing to a more equitable and inclusive society. While challenges remain in its implementation, concerted efforts to strengthen legal frameworks, extend protections to informal sector workers, promote gender-sensitive policies, and raise awareness can help realize the full potential of Article 42. Through these efforts, India can move closer to achieving true social and economic justice for all its citizens.

4. 2 - Government Strategies for Promoting Women's Education

4. 2. 1 - Beti Bachao Beti Padhao (BBBP)

Launched in 2015, the Beti Bachao Beti Padhao (BBBP) scheme is a flagship initiative of the Indian government aimed at addressing the declining child sex ratio and promoting the education of girls. This multi-sectoral program involves collaboration between the Ministry of Women and Child Development, the Ministry of Health and Family Welfare, and the Ministry of Education. At its core, BBBP seeks to transform societal attitudes towards girls, encouraging their education while ensuring their survival and protection. Since its inception, BBBP has made significant strides in increasing the enrollment of girls in schools and raising awareness about the importance of educating daughters.

1. Objectives of Beti Bachao Beti Padhao(BBBP): The primary objectives of Beti Bachao Beti Padhao are twofold: first, to address the issue of female foeticide and improve the declining child sex ratio, and second, to promote the education of girls. The program aims to achieve these objectives through a combination of advocacy, policy interventions, and community engagement. By targeting both the demand and supply sides of the issue, BBBP seeks to create an enabling environment where girls are valued, educated, and protected.

2. Multi-Sectoral Approach: BBBP adopts a multi-sectoral approach by involving multiple ministries and stakeholders in its implementation. The Ministry of Women and Child Development spearheads the program, coordinating efforts with the Ministry of Health and Family Welfare to address issues related to female foeticide and maternal health. The Ministry of Education plays a crucial role in promoting girls' education and ensuring their retention in schools. By leveraging the expertise and resources of these ministries, BBBP aims to achieve holistic outcomes that address the root causes of gender discrimination and inequality.

3. Changing Societal Attitudes: One of the key components of BBBP is its focus on changing societal attitudes towards girls. Deep-rooted cultural norms and preferences for sons have contributed to the skewed child sex ratio in India. BBBP seeks to challenge these norms by raising awareness about the value of girls and the importance of their education. Through media campaigns, community outreach programs, and grassroots initiatives, the program aims to shift perceptions and foster a more gender-equitable society where girls are seen as equal partners in development.

4. Promoting Girls' Education: Education is central to the Beti Bachao Beti Padhao initiative. By promoting girls' education, BBBP aims to empower them with knowledge, skills, and opportunities for socio-economic advancement. The program focuses on improving access to education for girls, especially in rural and marginalized communities, where gender disparities are most pronounced. Additionally, BBBP emphasizes the importance of girls' retention in schools, addressing barriers such as child marriage, socio-economic constraints, and lack of infrastructure.

5. Ensuring Survival and Protection: Beyond education, BBBP also aims to ensure the survival and protection of girls. This includes initiatives to address issues such as female foeticide, infant mortality, malnutrition, and violence against girls. The program promotes access to healthcare services, nutrition support, and legal protection for girls, with the goal of creating a safe and nurturing environment for their holistic development. By addressing these intersecting challenges, BBBP seeks to create a conducive ecosystem where girls can thrive and fulfill their potential.

6. Achievements and Impact: Since its launch, Beti Bachao Beti Padhao has achieved several significant milestones. The program has led to increased awareness about the importance of educating daughters and valuing the girl child. It has also contributed to improvements in the child sex ratio in many districts across the country. Moreover, BBBP has resulted in a significant rise in the enrollment of girls in schools, with more families recognizing the benefits of educating their daughters. These achievements underscore the transformative impact of BBBP in advancing gender equality and promoting girls' empowerment.

7. Challenges and Way Forward: While Beti Bachao Beti Padhao has made commendable progress, several challenges persist in its implementation. These include deep-rooted cultural beliefs, inadequate infrastructure, socio-economic disparities, and gaps in service delivery. Addressing these challenges requires sustained efforts at the grassroots level, strengthened coordination among stakeholders, and targeted interventions tailored to local contexts. Moreover, there is a need for continued monitoring and evaluation to track progress and identify areas for improvement.

Beti Bachao Beti Padhao stands as a testament to India's commitment to gender equality and girls' empowerment. Through its multi-sectoral approach and comprehensive strategies, BBBP has made significant strides in addressing the issues of female foeticide, skewed child sex ratio, and gender-based discrimination. By promoting girls' education, ensuring their survival and protection, and changing societal attitudes, BBBP has laid the foundation for a more equitable and inclusive society where every girl can realize her full potential. As the program continues to evolve, it is essential to build on its successes, address remaining challenges, and reaffirm the nation's collective resolve to empower every Beti (daughter) to Bachao (save) and Padhao (educate).

4. 2. 2 - National Scheme of Incentives to Girls for Secondary Education (NSIGSE)

The National Scheme of Incentives to Girls for Secondary Education (NSIGSE) is a pivotal initiative of the Indian government designed to promote secondary education among girls, especially those hailing from economically weaker sections and marginalized communities.

Launched with the overarching goal of reducing dropout rates and fostering a culture of educational attainment among girls, NSIGSE offers financial incentives to girls who successfully complete class VIII and enroll in class IX. This scheme plays a crucial role in mitigating financial constraints that often hinder girls' access to education beyond the primary level and underscores the nation's commitment to empowering girls through education.

Objectives of NSIGSE

The primary objective of the NSIGSE is to encourage girls, particularly from disadvantaged backgrounds, to continue their education beyond the primary level. By offering financial incentives, the scheme aims to address the socio-economic barriers that contribute to high dropout rates among girls in secondary education. Additionally, NSIGSE seeks to promote gender equality in education by providing equal opportunities for girls to pursue higher studies and unlock their full potential.

Target Beneficiaries

NSIGSE targets girls belonging to economically weaker sections, Scheduled Castes (SC), Scheduled Tribes (ST), and Other Backward Classes (OBC) communities, as well as those with disabilities. These groups are often disproportionately affected by poverty and face multiple barriers to accessing education, including lack of financial resources, social stigma, and inadequate infrastructure. By specifically targeting these marginalized communities, NSIGSE aims to address systemic inequalities and create pathways for social and economic empowerment.

Financial Incentives

Under the NSIGSE, eligible girls receive financial incentives upon completing class VIII and enrolling in class IX. The amount of the incentive varies depending on the state or union territory, with the central government providing financial assistance to cover a portion of the incentive amount. These incentives serve as a form of recognition for girls' academic achievements and provide tangible support to families grappling with the costs associated with education. By alleviating the financial burden, NSIGSE encourages families to prioritize girls' education and invest in their future.

Impact on Dropout Rates

One of the key outcomes of NSIGSE is its contribution to reducing dropout rates among girls in secondary education. By incentivizing enrollment and retention, the scheme ensures that girls are not forced to leave school due to financial constraints or other socio-economic factors. This has a ripple effect on girls' educational trajectories, as they are more likely to complete their secondary education and pursue higher studies. Moreover, NSIGSE fosters a sense of agency and empowerment among girls, encouraging them to aspire for academic excellence and socio-economic mobility.

Emphasis on Girls' Education

NSIGSE underscores the importance of prioritizing girls' education as a critical component of India's development agenda. By investing in girls' secondary education, the scheme lays the foundation for a more inclusive and equitable society where every girl has the opportunity to fulfill her potential. Moreover, NSIGSE aligns with global commitments to achieving gender equality and the Sustainable Development Goals (SDGs), particularly Goal 4 (Quality Education) and Goal 5 (Gender Equality).

Challenges and Way Forward

While NSIGSE has made significant strides in promoting girls' secondary education, several challenges remain in its implementation. These include issues related to awareness, outreach, and monitoring mechanisms. To address these challenges, there is a need for enhanced coordination among stakeholders, targeted interventions in underserved areas, and robust monitoring and evaluation systems to track progress and identify areas for improvement. Moreover, efforts should be made to address systemic barriers to girls' education, such as gender-based violence, early marriage, and lack of access to sanitation facilities.

The National Scheme of Incentives to Girls for Secondary Education (NSIGSE) exemplifies India's commitment to promoting girls' education and empowering them to realize their full potential. By offering financial incentives to girls from economically weaker sections and marginalized communities, NSIGSE addresses the socio-economic barriers that hinder their access to education. Moreover, the scheme contributes to reducing dropout rates, fostering gender equality, and advancing India's development goals. As NSIGSE continues to evolve, it is essential to build on its successes, address remaining challenges, and reaffirm the nation's resolve to create a more inclusive and equitable society where every girl has the opportunity to thrive and succeed.

4. 2. 3 - Kasturba Gandhi Balika Vidyalaya (KGBV)

The Kasturba Gandhi Balika Vidyalaya (KGBV) scheme, launched in 2004, stands as a beacon of hope for girls from disadvantaged backgrounds, particularly those belonging to Scheduled Castes, Scheduled Tribes, and Other Backward Classes. This transformative initiative aims to address the glaring gap in access to secondary education, especially in rural areas where educational opportunities for girls are limited. By establishing residential schools that provide free education, boarding, and lodging, the KGBV scheme seeks to empower girls with knowledge, skills, and confidence to pursue their dreams, unencumbered by societal barriers.

Objectives of KGBV

The primary objective of the KGBV scheme is to provide quality education and holistic development opportunities to girls from marginalized communities. By offering residential schooling facilities, the scheme aims to create a nurturing environment where girls can access education without facing the myriad challenges prevalent in their communities. Moreover, KGBV endeavors to bridge the gender gap in education by ensuring that girls receive the same opportunities as their male counterparts, thereby fostering gender equality and empowerment.

Target Beneficiaries

KGBV primarily targets girls from economically disadvantaged and socially marginalized backgrounds, including those belonging to Scheduled Castes, Scheduled Tribes, and Other Backward Classes. These communities often face systemic barriers to education, including poverty, cultural norms, and lack of infrastructure. By focusing on these vulnerable groups, KGBV aims to address the root causes of educational inequality and create pathways for social and economic empowerment. Additionally, the scheme prioritizes girls who are out of school or at risk of dropping out, providing them with a second chance at education and a brighter future.

Comprehensive Support System

One of the hallmarks of the KGBV scheme is its comprehensive support system, which goes beyond academic instruction to address the holistic needs of girls. In addition to providing free education, KGBV schools offer boarding and lodging facilities, nutritious meals, healthcare services, and extracurricular activities. This holistic approach ensures that girls receive the necessary support to thrive academically, emotionally, and socially. Moreover, by creating a conducive learning environment, KGBV empowers girls to break free from the cycle of poverty and transform their lives.

Bridging the Gender Gap

The KGBV scheme plays a pivotal role in bridging the gender gap in education by creating a supportive and inclusive learning environment for girls. By offering residential schooling facilities, the scheme addresses the unique challenges faced by girls in accessing education, including long distances to schools, safety concerns, and household responsibilities. Moreover, KGBV schools provide a space where girls can learn and grow without the fear of discrimination or gender-based violence, fostering a sense of belonging and empowerment.

Impact and Achievements

Since its inception, the KGBV scheme has made significant strides in improving access to education and empowering girls from marginalized communities. The establishment of KGBV schools has led to a substantial increase in the enrollment and retention of girls in secondary education, particularly in rural areas. Moreover, KGBV has contributed to improved learning outcomes, increased confidence and self-esteem among girls, and enhanced community participation in girls' education. These achievements underscore the transformative impact of KGBV in breaking down barriers to education and creating opportunities for girls to realize their full potential.

Challenges and Way Forward

While the KGBV scheme has been instrumental in advancing girls' education, several challenges persist in its implementation. These include issues related to infrastructure, teacher recruitment and training, monitoring and evaluation, and community participation. To address these challenges, there is a need for enhanced coordination among stakeholders, increased investment in infrastructure and human resources, and strengthened monitoring mechanisms to ensure accountability and transparency. Moreover, efforts should be made to address systemic barriers to girls' education, including poverty, child marriage, and social norms that prioritize boys' education.

The Kasturba Gandhi Balika Vidyalaya (KGBV) scheme embodies India's commitment to promoting girls' education and empowering them to break free from the cycle of poverty and inequality. By providing free education, boarding, and lodging to girls from marginalized communities, KGBV creates a supportive environment where girls can learn, grow, and thrive. Moreover, the scheme plays a pivotal role in bridging the gender gap in education, fostering gender equality and empowerment. As KGBV continues to evolve, it is essential to build on its successes, address remaining challenges, and reaffirm the nation's commitment to ensuring that every girl has the opportunity to fulfill her potential and contribute to India's progress and prosperity.

4. 2. 4 - Sarva Shiksha Abhiyan (SSA)

The Sarva Shiksha Abhiyan (SSA), translated as the Education for All Movement, stands as a cornerstone of India's educational landscape, representing a concerted effort by the government to universalize elementary education. Launched in 2001, SSA embodies a commitment to ensuring that every child, regardless of socio-economic background or gender, has access to quality education. Central to its mission is the empowerment of girls through education, reflecting a recognition of the transformative impact that education can have on individual lives and broader societal development.

Objectives of SSA

At its core, SSA seeks to improve access to quality education for all children, with a particular focus on marginalized and underserved communities. The program aims to ensure that every child receives a meaningful education that equips them with the knowledge, skills, and values necessary to thrive in an increasingly complex world. Moreover, SSA endeavors to promote equity and inclusivity in education, bridging the gap between urban and rural areas, and addressing disparities based on gender, caste, and socio-economic status.

Focus on Girls' Education

A key pillar of SSA is its emphasis on girls' education, recognizing the critical role that educated girls play in driving social and economic progress. To incentivize the enrollment and retention of girls in schools, SSA provides a range of support measures, including free textbooks, uniforms, and mid-day meals. These provisions not only alleviate the financial burden on families but also create a conducive environment for girls to pursue their education without facing barriers related to poverty or lack of resources.

Infrastructure Development

SSA places significant emphasis on infrastructure development, including the construction of school buildings, classrooms, and facilities such as libraries and laboratories. Of particular importance is the provision of separate toilets for girls, addressing a critical barrier to their participation in education. By ensuring access to safe and hygienic sanitation facilities, SSA seeks to create an environment where girls feel comfortable and secure, enabling them to attend school regularly and focus on their studies without concerns about privacy or dignity.

Community Participation and Ownership

A distinguishing feature of SSA is its emphasis on community participation and ownership in the planning, implementation, and monitoring of educational initiatives. Local communities, including parents, teachers, and village-level institutions, are actively involved in decision-making processes, ensuring that educational interventions are contextually relevant and responsive to local needs. This bottom-up approach not only fosters a sense of ownership and accountability but also strengthens the bonds between schools and the communities they serve, laying the foundation for sustainable and inclusive educational development.

Impact and Achievements

Since its inception, SSA has made significant strides in improving access to elementary education and promoting gender equality in schools. The program has led to a substantial increase in enrollment rates, particularly among girls from marginalized communities. Moreover, SSA has contributed to improved learning outcomes, reduced dropout rates, and increased community awareness about the importance of education. These achievements underscore the transformative impact of SSA in expanding educational opportunities and fostering social inclusion and empowerment.

Challenges and Way Forward

Despite its successes, SSA continues to face challenges in its implementation, including issues related to inadequate infrastructure, teacher shortages, and quality of education. Addressing these challenges requires sustained investment in human and financial resources, strengthening of monitoring and evaluation mechanisms, and targeted interventions to address systemic barriers to education. Moreover, there is a need for greater synergy and coordination among different levels of government and stakeholders to ensure effective implementation and maximize the impact of SSA.

The Sarva Shiksha Abhiyan (SSA) embodies India's commitment to ensuring that every child has access to quality education, regardless of their socio-economic background or gender. By prioritizing girls' education and promoting equity and inclusivity in education, SSA has played a pivotal role in expanding educational opportunities and driving social change. As India continues its journey towards achieving universal elementary education, SSA remains a beacon of hope, inspiring generations of children to dream, learn, and realize their full potential. Through continued investment, innovation, and collaboration, SSA will continue to shape the future of education in India and contribute to building a more inclusive and equitable society.

4. 2. 5 - Rashtriya Madhyamik Shiksha Abhiyan (RMSA)

The Rashtriya Madhyamik Shiksha Abhiyan (RMSA), also known as the National Mission for Secondary Education, emerged in 2009 as a pivotal initiative of the Indian government to elevate the quality and accessibility of secondary education across the nation. RMSA stands as a testament to India's commitment to nurturing the next generation of learners and preparing them for the challenges and opportunities of the 21st century. With a primary focus on enhancing access to secondary education and bridging the gender gap, RMSA aims to lay a strong foundation for equitable and inclusive educational development.

Objectives of RMSA

At its core, RMSA is driven by the overarching objective of achieving universal access to quality secondary education for all children, regardless of their socio-economic background or gender. The scheme seeks to ensure that every child completes at least eight years of schooling, as mandated by the Right to Education Act, and transitions seamlessly from primary to secondary education. Moreover, RMSA aims to enhance the quality of secondary education by improving infrastructure, enhancing teacher capacity, and promoting inclusive and learner-centered pedagogical practices.

Focus on Girls' Education

A central tenet of RMSA is its focus on promoting girls' education and reducing the gender gap in secondary education. Recognizing the critical role that secondary education plays in empowering girls and fostering their socio-economic advancement, RMSA sets ambitious targets to achieve a 100% enrollment rate for girls at the secondary level. To support this goal, the scheme implements a range of initiatives tailored to address the specific needs and challenges faced by girls, including providing scholarships, creating gender-sensitive learning environments, and offering life skills education.

Initiatives under RMSA

RMSA encompasses a diverse array of initiatives aimed at transforming secondary education and empowering learners. One such initiative is the provision of scholarships for economically disadvantaged students, including girls, to facilitate their access to education and alleviate financial barriers. Additionally, RMSA focuses on improving school infrastructure by constructing new classrooms, laboratories, libraries, and other facilities conducive to teaching and learning. Furthermore, the scheme emphasizes the professional development of teachers, equipping them with the knowledge and skills needed to address gender issues sensitively and create inclusive classrooms.

Preparation for Higher Education and Employment

By focusing on secondary education, RMSA plays a pivotal role in preparing students, particularly girls, for higher education and employment opportunities. Secondary education serves as a critical transition point in students' academic journey, laying the foundation for their future aspirations and endeavors. RMSA aims to equip students with the necessary academic, vocational, and life skills to pursue further studies or enter the workforce with confidence and competence. Moreover, by promoting girls' education at the secondary level, RMSA contributes to closing gender gaps in higher education and workforce participation.

Impact and Achievements

Since its inception, RMSA has made significant strides in expanding access to secondary education and improving its quality. The scheme has led to a substantial increase in enrollment rates at the secondary level, particularly among girls from marginalized communities. Moreover, RMSA has contributed to improved infrastructure, enhanced teacher capacity, and increased retention rates, ensuring that more students complete their secondary education. These achievements underscore the transformative impact of RMSA in advancing educational opportunities and fostering social inclusion and empowerment.

Challenges and Way Forward

Despite its successes, RMSA faces several challenges in its implementation, including issues related to infrastructure, teacher shortages, and quality of education. Addressing these challenges requires concerted efforts at both the policy and implementation levels, including increased investment in infrastructure and human resources, strengthened monitoring and evaluation mechanisms, and targeted interventions to address systemic barriers to education. Moreover, there is a need for greater collaboration and coordination among different stakeholders to ensure effective implementation and maximize the impact of RMSA.

The Rashtriya Madhyamik Shiksha Abhiyan (RMSA) exemplifies India's commitment to advancing secondary education and empowering learners to realize their full potential. By prioritizing girls' education and promoting equity and inclusivity in education, RMSA has played a pivotal role in expanding educational opportunities and driving social change. As India continues its journey towards achieving universal secondary education, RMSA remains a beacon of hope, inspiring generations of students to dream, learn, and contribute to the nation's progress and prosperity. Through continued investment, innovation, and collaboration, RMSA will continue to shape the future of education in India and pave the way for a more inclusive and equitable society.

4. 2. 6 - Digital Initiatives for Girls' Education

The Indian government has recognized the transformative potential of technology in promoting girls' education and has launched several digital initiatives to expand access to quality educational resources. At the forefront of this effort is the Digital India campaign, which aims to digitally empower citizens across the country, including girls from diverse socio-economic backgrounds. Through the Digital India initiative, girls are provided with access to information and communication technologies (ICTs), enabling them to overcome geographical barriers and access educational opportunities from anywhere, at any time.

SWAYAM and E-Learning Platforms

One of the flagship digital initiatives for girls' education is the SWAYAM (Study Webs of Active-Learning for Young Aspiring Minds) platform. SWAYAM offers a wide range of online courses and educational content across various subjects and disciplines, catering to the diverse learning needs and interests of girls. Through SWAYAM, girls can access high-quality educational resources, including video lectures, interactive assignments, and digital textbooks, thereby supplementing their traditional classroom learning with self-paced online study. Additionally, other e-learning platforms and digital repositories provide girls with access to a wealth of educational materials, empowering them to pursue their academic interests and aspirations.

Bridging the Gap in Educational Resources

Digital initiatives play a crucial role in bridging the gap in educational resources, particularly in remote and underserved areas where access to traditional educational infrastructure is limited. By leveraging technology, girls can access educational content and resources that may not be available locally, thereby expanding their learning horizons and enhancing their academic achievements. Moreover, digital initiatives facilitate collaborative learning and peer interaction, enabling girls to engage with educators and fellow learners from diverse backgrounds and communities.

Promoting Self-Directed Learning

Digital initiatives empower girls to take control of their learning journey and pursue education on their own terms. With the flexibility offered by online platforms, girls can tailor their learning experience to suit their individual preferences, pace, and learning styles. This promotes self-directed learning and fosters a sense of independence and autonomy among girls, empowering them to become lifelong learners and active participants in their educational journey. Additionally, digital platforms offer personalized learning experiences, adaptive assessments, and feedback mechanisms, thereby supporting girls' academic growth and development.

Overcoming Barriers to Education

Technology has the potential to overcome various barriers to education that girls may face, including geographical isolation, lack of educational infrastructure, and socio-cultural norms that restrict girls' mobility and access to formal schooling. Through digital initiatives, girls can access educational resources and participate in interactive learning experiences, irrespective of their physical location or socio-economic status. This democratization of education empowers girls to overcome traditional barriers and pursue their educational aspirations, thereby opening doors to new opportunities and pathways for socio-economic advancement.

Ensuring Inclusive and Equitable Education

Digital initiatives for girls' education are guided by principles of inclusivity and equity, ensuring that every girl has access to quality educational opportunities, regardless of her background or circumstances. Through targeted interventions and outreach programs, digital initiatives strive to reach marginalized and vulnerable groups, including girls from rural areas, low-income families, and minority communities. By addressing the digital divide and promoting digital literacy, these initiatives empower girls to participate fully in the digital age and unlock their potential as agents of change and innovation.

Digital initiatives have emerged as powerful tools for promoting girls' education and empowering them to realize their full potential. By leveraging technology, the Indian government is breaking down barriers to education and expanding access to quality educational resources for girls across the country. Through initiatives like SWAYAM and e-learning platforms, girls can access a wealth of educational content and engage in self-directed learning experiences that transcend traditional boundaries. As technology continues to evolve, digital initiatives hold the promise of transforming the landscape of girls' education, ensuring that every girl has the opportunity to learn, grow, and thrive in the digital age.

The constitutional provisions and government strategies outlined above underscore India's commitment to promoting women's education and achieving gender equality. Articles 14, 15(3), 39(d), and 42 provide a robust legal framework for ensuring equal opportunities for women in education and beyond. Government initiatives such as Beti Bachao Beti Padhao, NSIGSE, KGBV, SSA, and RMSA, along with digital initiatives, play a crucial role in addressing the barriers to girls' education and empowering women to reach their full potential. While significant progress has been made, continued efforts and investments are necessary to fully realize the vision of an inclusive and equitable educational landscape for all women in India.

4. 3 - Government Planning for Women's Education

To address the complex and multifaceted challenges faced by women in accessing education, the Indian government has developed various plans, policies, and commissions aimed at creating a more equitable and inclusive educational landscape. These efforts encompass strategic planning, policy formulation, and the establishment of dedicated institutions to oversee and promote women's education. Below, we explore some key components of government planning, including the National Plan of Action, the National Policy on Education, the National Health Policy, the National Commission for Women, and various educational commissions focused on women's education.

4. 3. 1 - National Plan of Action (NPA) for Education

The National Plan of Action (NPA) for Education stands as a comprehensive blueprint crafted to ensure the effective implementation of educational initiatives aimed at achieving universal access to education and enhancing its quality throughout the nation. Rooted in the principles of equity, inclusivity, and empowerment, the NPA encompasses a range of strategies and targets designed to address the diverse educational needs of all segments of society, with a particular emphasis on advancing women's education and fostering gender equality. Within the framework of the NPA, specific measures and interventions are outlined to promote the enrollment, retention, and academic success of girls across various levels of education.

Increasing Enrollment and Retention

A cornerstone of the NPA is its commitment to increasing the enrollment and retention rates of girls in schools, particularly in rural and marginalized communities where access to education remains a challenge. To achieve this objective, the NPA proposes a multifaceted approach that includes the provision of financial incentives, scholarships, and support services tailored to the specific needs of girls. By addressing socio-economic barriers and incentivizing girls' participation in education, the NPA aims to create a more inclusive and accessible educational landscape where every girl has the opportunity to pursue her academic aspirations.

Infrastructure Development

Recognizing the importance of creating a conducive learning environment, the NPA prioritizes infrastructure development in schools, with a particular focus on facilities that directly impact girls' education. This includes the construction of separate toilets for girls to ensure their privacy, dignity, and hygiene, thereby addressing a critical barrier to their attendance and retention in school. Additionally, the NPA emphasizes the provision of safe and reliable transportation options for girls, especially in rural areas where long distances and lack of transportation infrastructure pose challenges to accessing education.

Teacher Training and Curriculum Development

Another key aspect of the NPA is its emphasis on teacher training and curriculum development to promote gender sensitivity and inclusivity in the educational system. Through targeted capacity-building initiatives, teachers are equipped with the knowledge, skills, and attitudes needed to create a supportive and inclusive learning environment for girls. Furthermore, the NPA advocates for the integration of gender-inclusive content and perspectives into the curriculum, ensuring that educational materials reflect the diverse experiences and contributions of girls and women. By fostering a culture of gender equality and respect within schools, the NPA seeks to empower girls to reach their full potential and pursue their educational aspirations without constraints or discrimination.

The National Plan of Action (NPA) for Education represents a comprehensive and holistic approach to advancing women's education and promoting gender equality within the educational system. Through targeted interventions and strategic initiatives, the NPA aims to address the multifaceted barriers that hinder girls' access to education and inhibit their academic success. By prioritizing enrollment, retention, infrastructure development, teacher training, and curriculum development, the NPA lays the groundwork for a more inclusive, equitable, and empowering educational environment where every girl has the opportunity to thrive and succeed. As the implementation of the NPA progresses, it is essential to maintain momentum, monitor progress, and remain committed to the principles of gender equality and educational excellence, ensuring that the transformative potential of education is realized for all.

4. 3. 2 - National Policy on Education (NPE)

The National Policy on Education (NPE) serves as a foundational document guiding the development and implementation of educational initiatives in India. Originally formulated in 1968 and subsequently revised in 1986 and 1992, the NPE reflects the evolving educational priorities and aspirations of the nation. Central to the NPE is the recognition of the pivotal role of education in fostering social progress, economic development, and individual empowerment. Within this overarching framework, the NPE incorporates specific provisions aimed at promoting gender equality and empowering women through education, thereby reaffirming India's commitment to inclusivity and social justice.

Universal Access to Education

A fundamental objective of the NPE is to ensure universal access to primary education for all children, regardless of their socio-economic background or gender. Recognizing the historical disparities and systemic barriers that have hindered girls' access to education, the NPE prioritizes initiatives aimed at reducing gender disparities in enrollment, retention, and completion rates at the primary and secondary levels. By addressing structural inequalities and expanding educational opportunities, the NPE seeks to create a more inclusive and equitable educational landscape where every child, including girls, has the opportunity to realize their full potential.

Adult Education and Literacy

In addition to promoting universal access to formal education, the NPE underscores the importance of adult education and literacy programs in addressing the educational needs of women who missed out on formal schooling opportunities. Adult education initiatives, including literacy campaigns and vocational training programs, play a crucial role in enhancing women's literacy skills, empowering them to actively participate in economic and social life. By equipping women with the necessary knowledge and skills, adult education programs contribute to their personal development, economic empowerment, and overall well-being.

Equal Opportunities

The NPE advocates for equal opportunities in education for women, aiming to eliminate gender biases and discriminatory practices that may hinder girls' educational advancement. This includes addressing gender stereotypes and biases in textbooks, teaching methods, and educational materials to ensure that girls have access to inclusive and gender-responsive learning experiences. Moreover, the NPE emphasizes the importance of creating a supportive and enabling learning environment that encourages girls to pursue education and pursue their aspirations without fear of discrimination or prejudice.

The National Policy on Education (NPE) represents a comprehensive and forward-thinking approach to promoting gender equality and empowering women through education. By prioritizing universal access to education, adult education and literacy, and equal opportunities for women, the NPE lays the groundwork for a more inclusive, equitable, and empowering educational system. As India continues its journey towards achieving educational excellence and social justice, it is essential to uphold the principles and aspirations outlined in the NPE, ensuring that education remains a powerful instrument for transforming lives and building a more just and prosperous society for all.

4. 3. 3 - National Health Policy (NHP) 1983

The National Health Policy (NHP) 1983 stands as a seminal document shaping India's healthcare landscape, with a vision to ensure the provision of accessible, affordable, and equitable healthcare services to all segments of society. While primarily focused on health, the NHP 1983 acknowledges the intrinsic link between health and education, recognizing that education serves as a fundamental determinant of health outcomes, particularly for women. Within this framework, the NHP 1983 incorporates specific provisions aimed at promoting health education, improving access to healthcare services, and enhancing the overall well-being of women, thereby reinforcing the interconnectedness of health and education in fostering individual and societal development.

Health Education

A cornerstone of the NHP 1983 is its emphasis on health education as a powerful tool for improving health awareness and promoting healthy behaviors, particularly among women. Recognizing the pivotal role of education in shaping health-related attitudes and behaviors, the policy advocates for the integration of health education into the school curriculum, ensuring that students, especially girls, are equipped with the knowledge and skills needed to make informed decisions about their health and well-being. Moreover, the NHP 1983 calls for the implementation of awareness campaigns and community-based initiatives to disseminate information on key health issues such as nutrition, hygiene, and reproductive health, empowering women to take charge of their health and that of their families.

Access to Health Services

In addition to promoting health education, the NHP 1983 underscores the importance of improving access to healthcare services for women, particularly in the realm of maternal and child health care. Recognizing the critical role that maternal and child health plays in shaping women's overall well-being and their ability to pursue education, the policy advocates for the expansion of maternal and child health services, including prenatal care, safe delivery practices, and postnatal care. By ensuring access to quality healthcare services, the NHP 1983 seeks to address maternal and child mortality rates and enhance women's health outcomes, thereby creating conducive conditions for their educational attainment and socio-economic empowerment.

Intersecting Health and Education

The NHP 1983 underscores the intersecting nature of health and education, recognizing that improvements in health outcomes, particularly among women, can have a direct and positive impact on educational attainment and academic performance. Healthier women are more likely to attend school regularly, participate actively in learning activities, and perform better academically, thereby breaking the cycle of intergenerational poverty and promoting socio-economic development. By addressing the health needs of women and ensuring access to essential healthcare services, the NHP 1983 contributes to creating an enabling environment where women can fully realize their educational aspirations and contribute meaningfully to society.

The National Health Policy (NHP) 1983 embodies India's commitment to promoting health and well-being as essential prerequisites for individual and societal development. By recognizing the intersection of health and education, particularly for women, the NHP 1983 underscores the importance of integrating health education into the school curriculum, improving access to healthcare services, and addressing the health needs of women to promote their educational attainment and socio-economic empowerment. As India continues its journey towards achieving universal health coverage and equitable access to education, it is essential to uphold the principles and aspirations outlined in the NHP 1983, ensuring that health and education remain integral pillars of the nation's development agenda.

4. 3. 4 - National Commission for Women (NCW) 1990

Established in 1990, the National Commission for Women (NCW) stands as a pioneering institution dedicated to safeguarding and advancing the rights of women in India. Charged with the responsibility of promoting gender equality and addressing gender-based discrimination across various spheres of society, including education, the NCW plays a pivotal role in advocating for women's access to education and addressing systemic barriers to educational attainment. Through its multifaceted approach encompassing advocacy, policy recommendations, monitoring, and oversight, the NCW strives to create an enabling environment where girls and women can pursue education free from discrimination and inequality.

Advocacy and Policy Recommendations

Central to the mandate of the NCW is its role in conducting research, analysis, and advocacy to inform policy formulation and implementation in the realm of women's education. Leveraging its expertise and insights, the commission provides policy recommendations to the government aimed at addressing systemic barriers and promoting inclusive educational practices. By advocating for reforms and initiatives to eliminate gender-based discrimination in educational institutions, the NCW seeks to create a level playing field where girls and women can access quality education and realize their full potential.

Monitoring and Oversight

In addition to advocacy and policy recommendations, the NCW serves as a watchdog, monitoring the implementation of policies and programs designed to promote women's education and address gender disparities in educational outcomes. Through its monitoring and oversight functions, the commission ensures that educational institutions comply with legal provisions safeguarding women's rights and create a safe and inclusive learning environment for female students. Moreover, the NCW addresses grievances related to gender discrimination in education, providing a platform for women to seek redressal and recourse against instances of discrimination or harassment.

Empowering Women through Education

By championing women's access to education and advocating for gender-sensitive educational practices, the NCW contributes to empowering women and advancing gender equality in society. Education serves as a transformative force, enabling women to acquire knowledge, skills, and confidence to participate fully in social, economic, and political life. Through its efforts to address gender-based discrimination in education and promote inclusive educational policies and practices, the NCW plays a crucial role in breaking down barriers and creating opportunities for women to thrive and succeed in diverse spheres of life.

The National Commission for Women (NCW) stands as a beacon of hope and resilience in the journey towards gender equality and women's empowerment in India. Through its steadfast commitment to promoting women's access to education and addressing gender discrimination in educational institutions, the NCW contributes to creating a more equitable and inclusive society where every woman has the opportunity to fulfill her educational aspirations and realize her full potential. As India continues its quest for social justice and gender equality, the NCW remains a vital ally and advocate, steadfast in its mission to ensure that women's rights are protected, respected, and upheld in all facets of life, including education.

4. 4 - Various Educational Commissions on Women's Education

Throughout India's history, numerous educational commissions have been convened to examine and offer recommendations for improving women's education across the country. These commissions, comprising eminent scholars, educators, and policymakers, have played a pivotal role in shaping the trajectory of women's education and advocating for policies and reforms to address gender disparities in the educational landscape. Among the notable commissions that have focused on women's education are the University Education Commission, the Secondary Education Commission, the Kothari Commission, and the National Commission on Teachers, each of which has made significant contributions to advancing women's educational opportunities and promoting gender equality in the field of education.

4. 4. 1 - University Education Commission (1948-49)

Chaired by the distinguished philosopher and statesman Dr. S. Radhakrishnan, the University Education Commission underscored the importance of higher education for women and recommended the establishment of women's colleges and universities across India. Recognizing the transformative potential of higher education in empowering women and enhancing their socio-economic status, the commission advocated for the expansion of educational opportunities for women at the tertiary level, thereby laying the foundation for the establishment of numerous women's colleges and universities in subsequent years.

4. 4. 2 - Secondary Education Commission (1952-53)

Commonly known as the Mudaliar Commission, the Secondary Education Commission highlighted the need for special measures to promote girls' education at the secondary level, recognizing the pivotal role of secondary education in shaping women's future prospects and opportunities. In its recommendations, the commission emphasized the importance of developing vocational education programs tailored to the needs and aspirations of women, thereby equipping them with the skills and knowledge necessary for economic independence and social empowerment.

4. 4. 3 - Kothari Commission (1964-66)

The Kothari Commission, formally known as the Education Commission, emerged as a landmark initiative aimed at comprehensive educational reform in India. In addition to addressing broader issues of educational development, the commission dedicated considerable attention to enhancing women's education. Advocating for equal access to education for girls and boys, the commission championed the cause of co-education and called for the inclusion of women's studies in the curriculum, thereby laying the groundwork for a more inclusive and gender-sensitive educational system.

4. 4. 4 - National Commission on Teachers (1983-85)

The National Commission on Teachers highlighted the critical role of teachers in promoting gender equality and fostering a more equitable educational environment for girls. Recognizing the importance of teacher training on gender sensitivity and the development of gender-inclusive teaching practices, the commission emphasized the need for systematic efforts to enhance teachers' awareness of gender issues and equip them with the tools and resources to create a supportive and inclusive learning environment for all students, regardless of their gender.

The various educational commissions on women's education have played a crucial role in shaping India's educational landscape and advocating for policies and reforms to promote gender equality in education. From highlighting the importance of higher education for women to advocating for equal access to education and gender-sensitive teaching practices, these commissions have laid the groundwork for significant advancements in women's educational opportunities and empowerment. As India continues its journey towards achieving universal education and gender equality, the insights and recommendations of these commissions remain invaluable, serving as guiding principles for future policy interventions and initiatives aimed at advancing women's education and fostering a more inclusive and equitable educational system for all.

The Indian government's commitment to women's education is reflected in the numerous constitutional provisions, policies, and commissions dedicated to promoting gender equality in education. The National Plan of Action, the National Policy on Education, the National Health Policy, the National Commission for Women, and various educational commissions have all played significant roles in advancing women's education in India. These efforts have contributed to increased enrollment, retention, and achievement of girls in schools, while also addressing broader social and cultural barriers to women's education. Continued focus and investment in these areas are essential to ensure that all women in India have the opportunity to access quality education and achieve their full potential.

BIBLOGRAPHY

6. Ramachandran, Girls V. Women education: Policies and implementation mechanisms; case study: India. Bangkok: UNESCO. Principal Regional Office for Asia and the Pacific, 1998.
7. Bhat RA. Role of Education in the Empowerment of Women in India. Journal of Education and Practice. 2015;6(10):188-191.
8. Nyamidie JKE. African proverb of the month, 1999. Retrieved from: http://www. afriprov. org/index. php/african-proverb-of-the-month/25-1999proverbs/146-sep1999. html
9. Suguna M. Education and Women Empowerment in India. International Journal of Multidisciplinary Research, 2001, 1(8).
10. Oyitso M, Olomukoro OC. Enhancing women's development through literacy education in Nigeria. Review of European Studies. 2012;4(4):66-76.
11. Dominic B, Jothi CA. Education- A tool of Women Empowerment: Historical study based on Kerala society. International Journal of Scientific and Research Publications. 2012;2(4):2250-3153.
12. Raman SA. Women's education. Encyclopedia of India, 2006, 235–239.
13. Velkoff AV. Women of the world: Women's education in India, 1998. http://www. census. gov/population/international/files/wid-9801. pdf.
14. Sharmila N, Dhas CA. Development of women education in India. Munich Personal RePEc Archive, 2010.
15. Seth S. Gender and the nation: Debating female education. The western education of colonial India. Durham and London: Duke University Press, 2007, pp. 129-158.
16. Nair N. Women's education in India: A situational analysis. IMJ. 2010;1(4)
17. Harma J. Low cost private schooling in India: Is it pro poor and equitable? International journal of educational

development, 2011, 350-356.

18. Rose P. NGO provision of basic education: Alternative or complementary services delivery to support access to the excluded? Consortium for research on educational access, transitions and equity, 2007, 1-41.
19. Devi, A. B., &Jalandharachari, A. S. Growth Status of Adolescent Girls in Andhra Pradesh-a Case Study. MahilaPratishtha, 38. Retrieved on: 12 November, 2022 From:https://www.researchgate.net/profile/Uttam-Pegu/publication/352151085_Framing_women_as_Witches_2019/links/60bb283c92851cb13d79f408/Framing-women-as-Witches-2019.pdf#page=44
20. Devi, R., Gupta, S., &Verma, M. (2021). Awareness of women regarding BetiBachao and BetiPadhao scheme. International Journal of Home Science, 7(2), 181-183. Retrieved on:12November, 2022From:https://www.homesciencejournal.com/archives/2021/vol7issue2/PartC/7-2-57-998. pdf
21. Donoho, D. L., &Kipnis, A. (2022). Higher criticism to compare two large frequency tables, with sensitivity to possible rare and weak differences. The Annals of Statistics, 50(3), 1447-1472. https://projecteuclid. org/journals/annal s-of-statistics/volume-50/issue- 3/Higher-criticism-to-compare-two- large-frequency-tables-with- sensitivity/10. 1214/21-AOS2158. short
22. Dupin, C. M., &Borglin, G. (2020). Usability and application of a data integration technique (following the thread) for multi-and mixed methods research: a systematic review. International Journal of Nursing Studies, 108, 103608. Retrieved on: 12 November, 2022 From:https://www. sciencedirect. com/science/article/am/pii/S0020748920300 936
23. Fuhr, D. C., Weobong, B., Lazarus, A., Vanobberghen, F., Weiss, H. A., Singla, D. R., . . . & Patel, V. (2019). Delivering the Thinking

Healthy Programme for perinatal depression through peers: an individually randomised controlled trial in India. *The Lancet Psychiatry, 6*(2), 115-127. https://researchonline. lshtm. ac. uk/id/e print/4650192/2/Fuhr_2018_Delivering%20the%20Thinking %20Healthy%20Programme. pdf

24. Garg, N., & Singh, S. (2018). Financial literacy among youth. *International journaL of sociaLeconomics.* https://scholar. archive. org/work/kn5xogpnmrgs5m7nyknwfwosxm/access/wayback/ https://www. emerald. com/insight/content/doi/10. 1108/IJSE-11-2016- 0303/full/pdf?title=financial-literacy-among-youth
25. Ichsan, I. Z., Sigit, D. V., Miarsyah, M., Ali, A., &Suwandi, T. (2020). Implementation Supplementary Book of Green Consumerism: Improving Students HOTS in Environmental Learning. *EuropeanJournal of Educational Research9*(1), 227-237. https://files. eric. ed. gov/fulltext/EJ1241 204. pdf
26. Kanwal, S., (2022). Annual cost for higher education in India (2007-2018). *Statista.* Retrieved on 22nd September from https://www. statista. com/statistics/128 7401/india-annual-cost-of-higher- education-by-type/
27. Keddie, A. (2018). Adult education: An ideology of individualism. In *Adult education for a change* (pp. 45-64). Routledge. https://www. union. edu/sites/default/fil es/economics/202010/2019b-davis-williamson-ind-and-gender-world- development. pdf
28. Kumar, A. (2019). Social determinants of Mental Illness in India: An Empirical Study of Mental Ailment and Associated Social disquiets. International Journal of Research in Social Sciences, 9(4), 754-759. https://www. indianjournals. com/ijor. as px?target=ijor:ijrss&volume=9&issue=4 &article=045
29. Pellas, N., Fotaris, P., Kazanidis, I., & Wells, D. (2019).

Augmenting the learning experience in primary and secondary school education: A systematic review of recent trends in augmented reality game-based learning. Virtual Reality, 23(4), 329-346. Retrievedon:12 November, 2022 From: https://vbn.aau. dk/ws/files/293518026/M_ller_et_al_2018_European_Journal_of_Pain. pdf

30. Bhatta, T. P. (2018). Case study research, philosophical position and theory building: A methodological discussion. Dhaulagiri Journal of Sociology and Anthropology, 12, 72-79. Retrieved on:12November, 2022
31. Das, T. (2022). Status of Safety Conditions Of The Secondary School In The Light Of Rashtriya Madhyamik Shiksha Abhiyan (Rmsa). Agpe The Royal Gondwana Research Journal Of History, Science, Economic, Political And Social Science, 3(4), 116-124. Retrievedon:12November2022From:https://www.agpegondwanajournal. co. in/index. php/agpe/article/download/147/143
32. Agarwal, B., Anthwal, P., & Mahesh, M. (2021). How many and which women own land in India? Inter-gender and intra-gender gaps. *The Journal of Development Studies 57*(11), 1807-1829. From:https://www. nepjol. info/index. ph
33. Amrhein, V., Trafimow, D., & Greenland, S. (2019). Inferential statistics as descriptive statistics: There is no replication crisis if we don't expect replication. The AmericanStatistician, 73(sup1), 262-270. https://doi. org/10. 1080/00031305. 2018. 1543137
34. Atmowardoyo, H. (2018). Research methods in TEFL studies: Descriptive research, case study, error analysis, and R & D. Journal of Language Teaching and Research, 9(1), 197-204. Retrieved on: 12November, 2022From:http://academypublication. com/issues2/jltr/vol09/01/25. pdf
35. Barton, K. C. (2020). Students' understanding of institutional

practices: The missing dimension in human rights education. American Educational Research Journal, 57(1), 188217. Retrievedon:12November, 2022From:https://journals. sagepub. com/doi/pdf/10. 3102/0002831219849871

36. Bhat, R. A. (2015). Role of Education in the Empowement of Women in India. *Journal of Education and Practice, 6*(10), 188-191. https://files. eric. ed. gov/fulltext/EJ1081 705. pdf
37. Singh, S. P., &Ningthoujam, Y. (2022). Gender Wage Gap in Rural Labour Markets: An Empirical Study of North East India. The Journal of Asian Finance, Economics and Business, 9(6), 151-158. https://doi. org/10. 13106/jafeb. 2022. vo l9. no6. 0151
38. Statista Research Department (2022). Percentage of gender gap closed worldwide as of 2022, by dimension. Retrieved on 15th November 2022 from https://www. statista. com/statistics/121 2006/percentage-of-the-gender-gap- closed-worldwide-by-dimension/
39. Su, R., Stoll, G., & Rounds, J. (2019). The nature of interests: Toward a unifying theory of trait-state interestdynamics. In *Vocational interests in the workplace* (pp. 11-38). Routledge. Retrieved on: 12 November, 2022From:https://www. taylorfrancis. com/ch apters/edit/10. 4324/9781315678924-2/nature-interests-rong-su gundula- stoll-james-rounds
40. Upadhyaya., & Heena, R. (2010). Financing of higher education a case study of the M. S. University of Baroda
41. Choudhary, R. (2011). Case Studies of Women administrators: in Higher Education System of India
42. Jha, J., Ghatak, N., Menon, N., Dutta, P., & Mahendiram, S. (2019). Women's Education and Empowerment in Rural India.
43. Srivatsan, A., & Srivatsan , A. (2020). Shining Light in Women's education
44. Tim, A., & Stephanie, S. (2021). Femininity and the History of Women's Education.

45. Agarwal, B., Anthwal, P., & Mahesh, M. (2021). How many and which women own land in India? Inter-gender and intra-gender gaps. The Journal of Development Studies, 57(11), 1807-1829.
46. https://www. tandfonline. com/doi/pdf/10. 1080/00220388. 2021. 1887478 Agarwal, B., Anthwal, P., & Mahesh, M. (2021).
47. How many and which women own land in India? Inter-gender and intra-gender gaps. The Journal of Development Studies, 57(11), 1807-1829.
48. https://www. tandfonline. com/doi/pdf/10. 1080/00220388. 2021. 1887478

www.ingramcontent.com/pod-product-compliance
Lightning Source LLC
LaVergne TN
LVHW031343150826
845673LV00009B/2838

* 9 7 8 9 3 4 8 3 3 2 9 4 3 *